The Pocket Book of
Adobe Acrobat 8 Professional

Andy Zhang

 **Champion Writers**

The Pocket Book of
Adobe Acrobat 8 Professional
First Edition
Copyright © 2008 by Andy Zhang

International Standard Book Number: 978-1-4196-8836-2

Printed in the United States of America.

Trademark Notice

Adobe® and Acrobat® are registered trademarks of Adobe Systems Incorporated. Champion Writers cannot attest to the accuracy of this information.

Disclaimer

The author of this book is not affiliated with Adobe Systems Incorporated and/or its affiliates. Therefore, the views and opinions expressed in this book do not represent the views and opinions of Adobe Systems Incorporated and/or its affiliates.

The information presented in this book is for reference only. The author(s) and publisher strive to provide accurate information. Several factors will create different user experiences than the one presented in this book. These factors include variations of software versions, patches, operating systems, configurations, and customizations. This book is not warranted to be error-free or up-to-date.

Reference resources listed in this book, such as Web site addresses, may have changed after this book was published.

The author(s) and the publisher shall have neither liability nor responsibility to any person or entity with respect to any loss or damages arising from the information contained in this publication.

for Michelle

We Love to Hear from You!

Every reader of this book has something to say that we may learn from. Your opinions and comments are invaluable to us. While every precaution has been taken in the preparation of this book, there remains the possibility that errors or omissions still exist. If you find errors or omissions in this book, please check out the publisher's Web site and review all documented errata. If you do not find your issue on that list, please submit your comments to us, and we will update our Web site and correct all of the known issues in the next release.

Please note that the author(s) is unable to help you with any technical issues related to the topics included in this book. Due to the volume of messages we receive from our readers, we are unable to respond to every message; however, please be assured that your message will be carefully read, considered, and provided with a response when warranted.

When contacting us, please visit publisher's Web site at:

http://www.championwriters.com

Contents at a Glance

Table of Contents

Conventions Used in This Book

The following conventions are used in this book:
Italic is used for:
- Program Names, pathnames, and filenames
- Web addresses (URLs)
- Book or article titles

Constant Width is used for:
- Source code examples
- SQL statements

Bold is used for
- Emphasis
- Menu item or command

Please pay attention to the following icons:

 Warning: this message should be carefully reviewed to prevent issues or problems.

 Tips: This message provides you some shortcuts or efficient ways to solve problems.

 Real World: Real world working experience summary for the related topic.

1

Introduction to Adobe Acrobat 8 Professional

Welcome to Adobe Acrobat 8 Professional! In this chapter, we are going to cover a few different features; you can open a sample PDF document to follow along. If you have not installed Adobe Acrobat 8 Professional, you can use Appendix I as your installation guide.

We start this chapter with the standard Acrobat workspace. During this section, we will discuss: 1) workspace layout; 2) floating and docking toolbars; 3) splitting windows; 4) displaying grids and rulers; 5) viewing page thumbnails; 6) panning and zooming; and 7) switching to full screen mode.

Knowing Your Workspace Layout

There are four major functional areas in your Adobe Acrobat 8 Professional workspace: menu, toolbars, navigation pane, and document pane. The menu contains features you use to work with your document. Toolbars can be customized, and here you can find some of the most frequently used features. The navigation pane helps you to move around within the document, find attachments, search for help topics, and more.

The document pane contains your document content and is where you will perform most of your work.

Figure 1-1

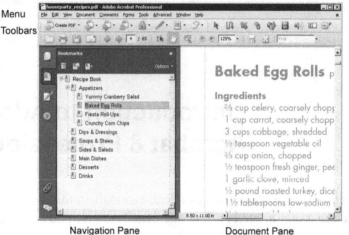

Navigation Pane   Document Pane

Floating and Docking Toolbars

There are two states of a toolbar—floating or docked. Floating toolbars can be moved around inside your workspace and docked toolbars will be positioned at the toolbar area. You can always dock a floating toolbar by dragging it to the toolbar region. There are many toolbars available and you can choose the one you need by going to menu option **Tools → Customize Toolbars → More Tools**. From this window, you can select or deselect the tools you want and customize your workspace.

Figure 1-2

Splitting Windows

You can split your document window into two or four document panes (spreadsheet split). To split your window, go to **Windows → Split** (or **Windows → Spreadsheet Split**).

Figure 1-3

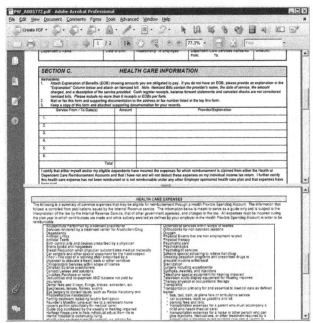

Displaying Grids and Rulers

When you work with documents that require more precision, it is useful to have grids turned on. To show grids, go to **View → Grid** or use the shortcut keys **[Ctrl + U]** in Windows or **[Command + U]** in Mac OS.

Figure 1-4

To change your grid appearances such as line color or width, go to **Edit Preferences** in Windows or **Acrobat → Preferences** in Mac OS. Inside the Preferences window, select **Units & Guides**. The Layout Grid pane will be on the right.

Figure 1-5

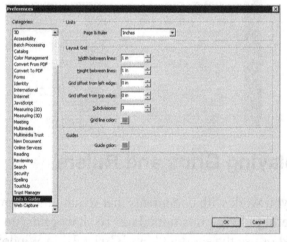

You may also find it useful to display rulers in your document area. To show rulers, go to **View → Rulers** or use the shortcut keys [**Ctrl + R**] in Windows or [**Command + R**] in Mac OS.

> Grids and rulers may also be disabled by the same method used to display them.

Figure 1-6

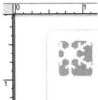

Viewing Page Thumbnails

The Page Thumbnail navigation pane is very useful when working on a large document. You can scroll, print, insert, extract, delete, rotate, replace pages, and much more! From the Options menu, you can also enlarge or reduce the page thumbnail size.

Figure 1-7

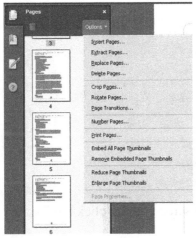

Panning and Zooming

If you want to maneuver through your document easily and zoom in or out quickly, the Pan and Zoom window is your friendly tool. You can move around the document areas, zoom in and out, and navigate to different pages using this tool.

Figure 1-8

Switching to Full Screen Mode

If you need to view your document in full screen mode for presentations or other reasons, go to **Windows → Full Screen Mode** or use the shortcut keys [**Ctrl** + **L**] in Windows or [**Command** + **L**] in Mac OS.

Figure 1-9

 To leave full screen mode, click the **Esc** key.

Getting Started Window

When you first log on to Adobe Acrobat 8 Professional, you will see the flash screen with task-based buttons linked to commonly used features, including create PDF, combine files, export, start meeting, secure, sign, forms, and review & comment.

If you don't want this window to show every time you open
Adobe Acrobat, select the **Do not show at startup** option on
the top right-hand corner of the window.

If for any reason you don't see this window and would like to
see it, go to **Help → Getting Started with Adobe Acrobat 8
Professional** to see this window. You also can deselect the **Do
not show at startup** option to make sure this window comes
up when you open Adobe Acrobat.

Figure 1-10

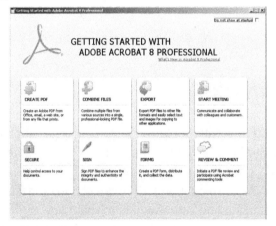

Using the Organizer

If you want to view the documents you have viewed recently,
open the organizer. The organizer shows you the working
history of your PDF documents. You also can print, e-mail to
some recipients, combine files, organize files into collections,
and send files for review. It is a convenient portal to accomplish
many tasks. To open your organizer, go to **File → Organizer
→ Open Organizer,** or use the shortcut key [**Shift + Ctrl + 1**]
in Windows or [**Shift + Command + 1**] in Mac OS.

Figure 1-11

Bookmarks

If you want to create bookmarks for your PDF documents, open the bookmarks navigation pane. To create a new bookmark, click on the New Bookmark button; then name your bookmark. When you are ready to set the page destination for your bookmark, you can navigate to that page, right click on the bookmark you need, and select Set Destination from the popup menu.

Figure 1-12

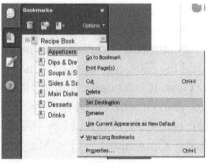

Setting Bookmark Hierarchy

To set a "bookmark nest" under another (parent) bookmark, first create a new bookmark and then drag and drop the bookmark below the parent bookmark. You should see a dotted line below the parent bookmark.

Figure 1-13

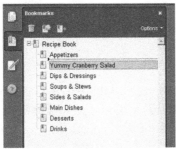

Once you release your mouse button, the bookmark is nested. If this is the "first child" bookmark, the parent bookmark should now have a plus sign in front of it. Once you expand the parent bookmark, the plus sign becomes minus sign.

Figure 1-14

Add Another Child Bookmark

To add more child bookmarks under the same parent, click on the New Bookmark button with the current child bookmark selected. The new bookmark will be automatically added under the same parent.

Move Child Bookmark Out of Nest

To move your child bookmark out of the current nest, drag it to the appropriate position, and it will be positioned at its new location. Building a bookmark tree structure is an easy process.

Links

You can find the link button from the Advanced Editing toolbar. If you don't see this toolbar, go to **Tools → Customize Toolbars**, and then select the Advanced Editing toolbar.

Figure 1-15

With your link button selected, you can position your link area at your desired document location. You should see the Create Link window with various link options.

Figure 1-16

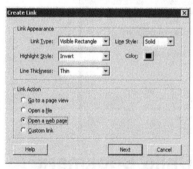

If you choose to link to a Web page, type the Web address (URL) into the textbox. If you choose to link to a document, you can browse to locate the document, and then set the Open Window preferences.

Figure 1-17

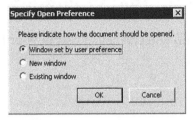

Select Document Elements

Select and Copy a Portion of a Page

With Acrobat Professional 8, you can take a snapshot of your page or select and copy a portion of your page. To take a snapshot, go to **Tools → Select & Zoom**, and then select the **Snapshot Tool**. If your selected area is a block of text, the text is copied to the clipboard as soon as your selection is complete, and from there, you can copy your text to other applications. If your selected area is an image or a portion of an image, you can copy the image or portion thereof to other applications as well.

Figure 1-18

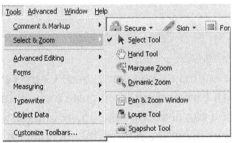

Inside other applications, you can use **Edit → Paste** to bring the snapshot text or image into that application.

Select and Copy Text or Images

With the selection tool, you can select text in your PDF document.

Figure 1-19

To select text, drag your mouse pointer across the text area or image, and your selected text or image will be highlighted. If text has not been selected, multiple clicks near the text will allow you to select a word, a line of text, or the entire document. With your text block or image selected, you can access many menu options when you right-click and trigger the pop-up menu.

Figure 1-20

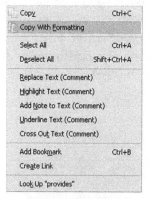

To copy text or an image, you can choose **Copy Text** or **Copy Text With Formatting**, then paste the text into other applications. You can also copy the image and paste it into other applications using the pop-up menu. Alternatively, you can drag and drop your image into other applications while the image is selected.

To select all text and images inside a document, you can use **Edit → Select All**. In Windows, you can also use **Ctrl + A**. In

Mac OS, you can use **Command** + **A**. Alternatively, you can click on your PDF document four times.

Select, Copy, and Save Tables

You can use the **Select Tool** to select rows and columns within a table or the entire table. Once your table has been selected, you can right-click to trigger the pop-up menu. You can then select the **Open Table in Spreadsheet** option to open it in Excel, or you can drag and drop your table into another application. If that application, such as Word, supports the Rich Text Format, your table format will be maintained in Rich Text. To copy your table, select the **Copy as Table** option.

Figure 1-21

Inside Excel, you can use **Edit → Paste Special** to open up the **Paste Special Dialog Box**. If you select **Paste as XML Spreadsheet**, your table format should be retained in Excel.

Figure 1-22

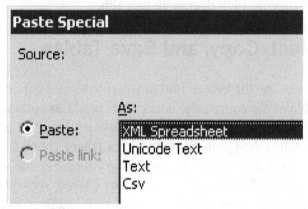

With your table selected, you can also choose **Save as Table** to save your table into a file. Your table can be saved as Comma Separated Values (*.csv), HTML 4.01 with CSS 1.0 (*.htm, *.html), Rich Text Format (*.rtf), Text (Tab Delimited) (*.txt), Unicode Text (Tab Delimited) (*.txt), XML 1.0 (*.xml), and XML Spreadsheet (*.xml).

Figure 1-23

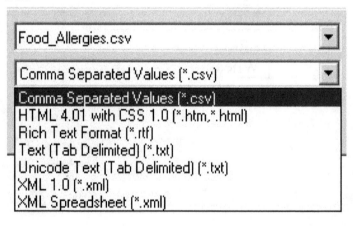

Select, Copy, and Save Images

To select an image, simply click on the image. Alternatively, you can use the mouse pointer to draw a rectangular shadow around the entire image or portion thereof. Please note that you can draw a rectangular shadow only when your mouse pointer has turned into a crosshair pointer.

Figure 1-24

You may also able to see the **Copy Image** icon.

Figure 1-25

When you are ready to copy or save your image, right-click on the image and trigger the pop-up menu. You should see both the **Copy Image [Ctrl + C]** and **Save Image As**... options. After you click on **Copy Image** or use shortcut keys [**Ctrl + C**], you can paste your image in other applications. Alternatively, you can go to **Edit → Copy** to copy your image.

When you select the **Save Image As**... option, you can save your image as a bitmap image file, TIFF image file, or a JPEG image file.

Figure 1-26

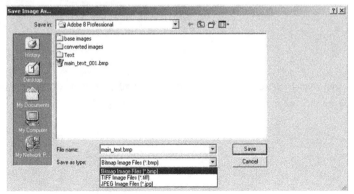

Creating Article Threads

When you are working with a PDF document for a newspaper or a magazine, it is likely that your article flows from column to column and occasionally jumps to a different page. To avoid confusing your reader, you can use the article tool to create an article thread. An article thread helps your readers follow the article flow without being lost. The article thread tool is available from the **Advanced Editing Toolbar**. If you don't see this toolbar, you can go to **Tools → Customize Toolbars...** and then select the article tool.

Figure 1-27

Once the article tool is selected, you can select areas of the article and sequentially number each article area. You can repeat the process until you have completed the entire article flow.

Figure 1-28

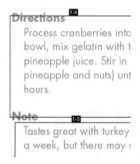

Once you have completed the article flow, you can add article properties in the **Article Properties Window**.

Figure 1-29

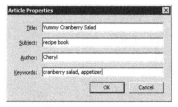

Update Your Profile

If you would like to update your profile information, you can go to **Edit → Preferences** in Windows, or go to **Acrobat →** **Preferences** in Mac OS to edit your preferences, including personal identity information.

Figure 1-30

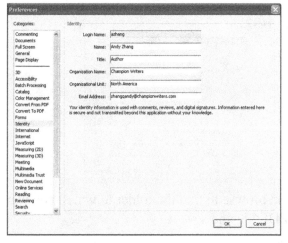

Print Ready Files

To define your PDF document settings, you can go to **Advanced → Print Production**, then select **PDF Job** **Definitions** or you can use **PDF Job Definitions** from the **Print Production Toolbar**.

Figure 1-31

Also, from the Create New Job Definition Window, you can either create a new print definition file or create print definitions based on a document.

Figure 1-32

You can browse to find the folder to which you want to save your PDF file and save it.

Figure 1-33

Once you have your PDF file defined, you can edit or submit the PDF file.

Figure 1-34

When you edit your PDF Job definitions, you can modify both general and customer information.

Figure 1-35

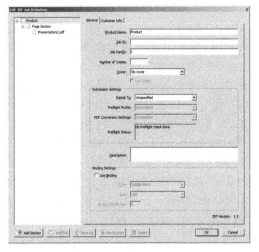

Under the **General Tab**, you can specify submission settings, including preflight profile and binding properties. Under the **Customer Information Tab**, you can enter billing, customer, and job information.

Summary

In this chapter, we introduced the Adobe Acrobat 8 Professional workspace and some of the essential skills needed to work with your PDF document. Within your workspace, you can configure how toolbars are positioned, add and remove toolbars according to your needs, split windows into either two or four windows, display grids and rulers for layout precision, navigate through pages with page thumbnails and navigation panes, view your document in full screen mode, pan and zoom within your document, and enable or disable the **Getting Started Window**.

We also introduced Organizer—a handy tool to review your work history and organize files. Later, we covered bookmarks and links. We also discussed how to select and copy a portion of a document page, text, image, and table. Additionally, we discussed creating article threads, which can keep readers in the correct article flow of a magazine or newspaper article. Lastly, we covered how to update user profiles and create print ready files. Please note that user profile information is useful in many areas with Adobe Acrobat 8 Professional, especially when sharing documents, providing comments, and submitting reviews. So, you should take time to update the user profile.

2

Creating PDF Document

In 1990, Portable Document Format (PDF) became one of the most successful creations during the Internet boom. HTML web pages can be viewed and printed from web browsers, but the print results are very dependent on the browser type and version, printer settings, and other environment properties. Its use and flexibility is further compounded by frames, special characters (such as mathematical symbols), background colors, server and client side scripts, and style sheets. Users demand a dependable and consistent way of sharing information across different operating systems, web browsers, and applications. PDF documents provide users with the ability to print, view the same document with the same results, regardless of what the end user's computing environment differences may be. It is a convenient and reliable way of sharing documents.

Because Adobe PDF reader is free to download, it soon became an indispensable application to almost all Internet users. Adobe Acrobat, the development environment for creating PDF documents, also made impressive progress since then—allowing users to create PDF documents from a wide variety of applications, plus it added many popular features such as mail merge, comments, and meetings.

In this chapter, we are going to introduce you to how to create

PDF documents using Adobe Acrobat 8 Professional from many applications. Once you have successfully installed Adobe Acrobat 8 Professional, you should be able to see Acrobat menus and shortcut menu icons in applications that are supported by Adobe Acrobat. If you have not installed Acrobat Professional 8, use Appendix I as your installation reference guide.

When you first log into Adobe Acrobat 8 Professional, you will see the flash screen with task-based buttons linked to commonly used features including: create PDF, combine files, export, start meeting, secure, sign, forms, and review & comment.

Creating PDF Document from Microsoft Office

Microsoft Office applications are frequently used for creating PDF documents. Creating PDF files from Microsoft Office applications often require only one click of the **Convert to Adobe PDF** button. In this section, we will show you how to create PDF files from various Microsoft Office applications including Word, Excel, PowerPoint, and Project.

 Please note that if you are using Microsoft Office 2007 applications and you have Acrobat Processional 8.0, you should download and install Adobe Acrobat 8.1 SDK (or the latest SDK). Currently, the download web site address is:

http://www.adobe.com/devnet/acrobat/.

Creating PDF Document from Microsoft Word

Microsoft Word is an application packed with many writing and formatting tools. Prior to Word 2007, all Word documents ended with .doc file extension. In Word 2007, documents end with .docx extension. You can create backward compatible versions of your Word document with .doc file extension, but you can't open .docx documents in the previous version of Microsoft Word.

Figure 2-1

After you have opened your Word document, you can use either use the **Convert to Adobe PDF** menu sub item from **Adobe PDF** menu or use the shortcut button as shown in Figure 2-2.

Figure 2-2

You should see the **Creating Adobe PDF** progress bar while converting to a PDF document from Word.

Figure 2-3

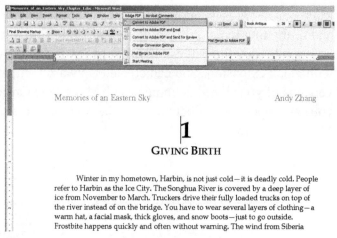

Figure 2-4

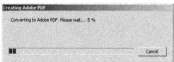

Once your document is created in PDF, it automatically opens in Adobe Acrobat Professional.

Figure 2-5

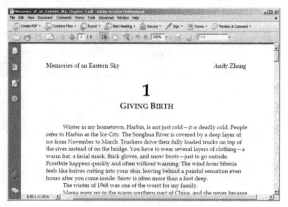

Creating PDF Document from Microsoft Excel

Microsoft Excel has become one of the most popular applications to share, present, and analyze data. Acrobat Professional 8 can convert Excel worksheets into PDF documents and retain the position, colors, and dimensions for different types of charts within the worksheet. To create PDF documents from Excel, you can use either use the **Convert to Adobe PDF** menu sub item from the **Ado_be PDF** menu or use the shortcut button.

Figure 2-6

Creating PDF documents from Excel worksheets can make document sharing and printing a simple task. Even if the user does not have Microsoft Office installed, they can print and use your Excel spreadsheet chart and data from the PDF you create and send.

Figure 2-7

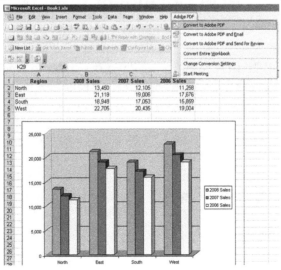

You may need to adjust your worksheet column widths or chart positions to ensure the PDF document looks satisfactory to you. Once you have generated a PDF document from your Excel worksheet, you can find dotted lines in your worksheet— helping you to determine the available space in a PDF document page.

Figure 2-8

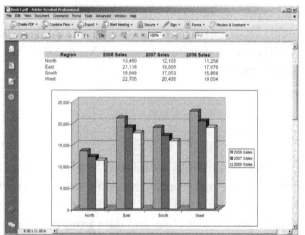

Creating PDF Document from Microsoft PowerPoint

Creating PDF files from PowerPoint is similar to creating a PDF document from Word or Excel. It is as simple as a click of a button.

Please note: Each PowerPoint slide will be created as an individual page in the PDF document. Even if you create the PDF document from Slide Sorter View, the PDF document will be created with individual slide pages.

Figure 2-9

You can view your PDF document as soon as your PowerPoint slides have been converted.

Figure 2-10

Creating PDF Document from Microsoft Project

You can create PDF document from Microsoft Project using either the **Convert to PDF** button or the **Adobe PDF** menu. If your Project document has more information than one PDF document page, then the remaining document will automatically flow onto the next page. For example, converting a Gantt chart often requires additional PDF pages.

Figure 2-11

Creating PDF Document from Microsoft Visio or AutoCAD

In AutoCAD, you can select layers, define page size, and preserve layout for the PDF file you are creating. Another advance of Adobe Acrobat 8 Professional is the faster speed of creating PDF files from AutoCAD. Inside AutoCAD you can select or deselect the layers you want to include in your PDF document. To create a PDF document from AutoCAD or Visio, you can use either **Convert to Adobe PDF** menu sub item from **Adobe PDF** menu or use the shortcut button.

Figure 2-12

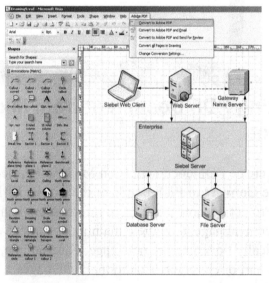

Acrobat PDFMaker will ask if you want to include "Custom Properties" of the shapes in the created Adobe PDF. This option is selected by default. When you include Custom Properties, you can then select an object in the PDF document by using the Object Data tool to view Custom Properties.

Figure 2-13

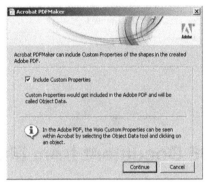

You have three options: 1) flattening all layers—combining all layers into one; or 2) retain all layers; or 3) retain some layers in the selected page. If you always want to flatten layers, you can check "Always flatten layers and don't show this dialog again" to speed up PDF generating process in the future.

Figure 2-14

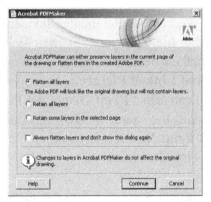

Once you have completed your selection, your confirmation screen should come up. When you click on the **Convert** button, your PDF document will then be created.

Figure 2-15

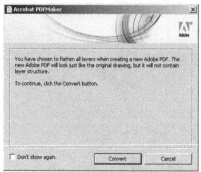

Creating PDF Document from Microsoft Publisher

Most people use Publisher to design print materials such as newsletters, flyers, and brochures. To create a PDF document from Publisher, you can use either the **Convert to Adobe PDF** menu sub item from the **Adobe PDF** menu or use the shortcut button.

If you have moved your embedded images since the time you created your Publisher file, then you will see a dialog box pop up and ask you to make a decision regarding the missing link. You can click on **Find Linked Picture...** to browse and locate your picture, or you can select **Print Displayed Picture** to use the displayed picture as the source image to generate your PDF document, or select **Print No Picture** to skip the pictures that are missing from their linked location.

Once your PDF document is created, you can view it in Acrobat Professional.

Figure 2-16

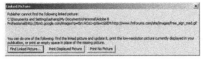

 I was impressed by the quality of the PDF files created from Publisher by Acrobat Professional 8 because it maintained the page size, font, image scale, and position.

Creating PDF Document from a Web Page

Acrobat Professional 8 gives you the capability to navigate to a web site, then create a PDF document for either the entire web site or a single web page. With this feature, you can store and archive web pages into PDF documents.

First, you either type your destination URL into the URL textbox directly, or use the **Browse** button to browse to the web site. You can also arrange your settings such as how many levels are needed to get the web site, or you can choose to **Get entire site.** You can also choose to **Stay on same path** to remain on the same web site file directory, or **Stay on same server** to download web pages only in a particular server.

Figure 2-17

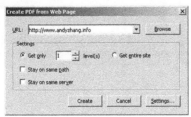

Once you finished your settings, you can start to create your PDF document. You should see a download status screen while Acrobat Professional is retrieving the web page data.

Figure 2-18

Your PDF document will be created once the entire process is completed. You can see that the document title is taken from the web page title tag and your PDF document should look like the source web page.

Figure 2-19

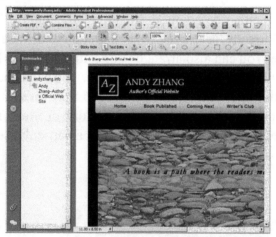

Creating PDF Document from Outlook or Lotus Notes

You can archive your e-mails into PDF documents that retain the layout and document content of your e-mail application whether it is Outlook or Lotus Notes. Because most of us receive many e-mails throughout the course of a day, most e-mail servers have limited storage for individual accounts. Creating PDF documents for important e-mails can save your time plus the valuable storage space on your e-mail server. You can use the archive function to collect your e-mails, but PDF documents can be viewed without using your e-mail applications such as Outlook or Lotus Notes. PDF serve as one more option in saving your e-mails for search, backup, and retrieval.

Creating PDF documents from Outlook or Lotus Notes is similar to creating a PDF document from other applications, which we discussed earlier. Once your e-mail PDF document has been created, you can see the file path, subject, date, size, and other e-mail properties, along with your actual PDF file in Adobe Acrobat 8 Professional.

Figure 2-20

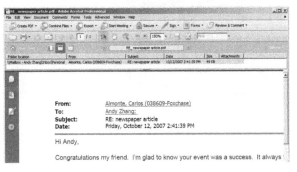

You can also send your created PDF document as an e-mail attachment.

Figure 2-21

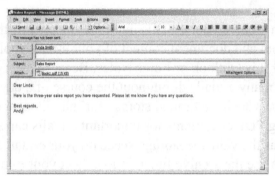

Creating PDF Document from Paper Document

You can also create PDF documents from an external device such as a scanner. Once you have selected your input device, you can then select the output method: either creating a new PDF document or appending to an existing PDF. Then scan your paper document in the scanner.

Figure 2-22

Creating PDF Document from Clipboard Image

You can create a clipboard image by pressing the **Print Screen** key to capture the entire screen space or **Alt + Print Screen** to capture the active window in Windows Operating Systems. In Mac OS, you can use the **Grab** utility and click on **Capture**, then select from **Selection, Window, Screen**, or **Timed Screen**.

In Windows, you can create a PDF document after you have captured your clipboard image. Once your clipboard is stored with an image, you can go to **File → Create PDF → From Clipboard Image**. Your clipboard image will be created as a PDF document and it will be displayed inside active workspace.

Figure 2-23

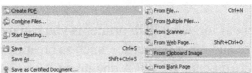

In Mac OS, you can start from **File → Create PDF → From Clipboard Image,** then use the **Grab** utility to capture your screen. Acrobat Professional 8 will automatically create a PDF document for you. Once your PDF document is created, it will open in your Acrobat active workspace.

Creating PDF Document from PDF Printer

You can also create a PDF document from a PDF printer. You should be able to locate your PDF printer among your printers from many applications.

Figure 2-24

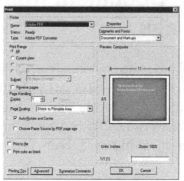

Once you click on **Print**, PDF printer will create your document in PDF format.

Figure 2-25

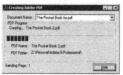

Another benefit for using PDF printer is you can modify the page size and other properties, such as creating PDF/A-compliant documents. A PDF/A document is a subset of a PDF document that is geared for long-term archiving purposes. Within a PDF/A document, all features that are not appropriate for archive have been stripped out of it.

Figure 2-26

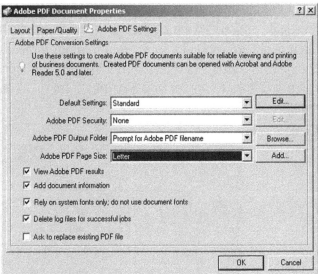

Drag and Drop

In Windows OS with Acrobat Professional 8 opened, you can drag and drop your file into the active workspace window. Acrobat Professional 8 will create a PDF document for you.

If you are using Mac OS, simply drag and drop your file icon onto the Acrobat Professional 8 icon and you will accomplish the same task.

This feature is especially useful when you work with applications that have no menu options or shortcut buttons for creating PDF documents directly. For example, you can drag and drop a plain text document created in Notepad to create your PDF document. Also, you can use PDF printer to create a PDF document from these applications.

Changing Conversion Settings

At times, you may want to change the way your PDF documents are created. If you want to modify the default conversion settings before creating your PDF document, you can use **Change Conversion Settings** from the **Adobe PDF** menu.

Figure 2-27

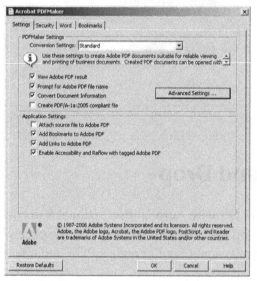

For many organizations and document archive specialists, they need to ensure that all documents follow their individualized compatibility standards. To set compatibility standards and other options, you can click on the **Advanced Settings...** button.

At the **Settings** screen, you can set compatibility to previous versions of Acrobat. By default, it sets to Acrobat 5.0 (PDF 1.4). You can also set compression level, page size, font and color properties, binding, resolution, and other settings.

Figure 2-28

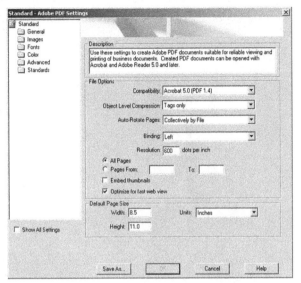

Summary

In this chapter, we covered the process of creating PDF document from various applications including Microsoft Word, Excel, PowerPoint, and Publisher. We discussed how to create a PDF document from Visio or AutoCAD, web page, Outlook, or Lotus Notes. If you find that the default settings for creating PDF documents need to be modified, you can change conversion settings before you create the document.

In addition, we covered how to create a PDF document from a paper document by using an external device, such as a scanner. You can also create a PDF document from a clipboard image. You can use PDF printer or the drag and drop method to create PDF documents. This is immensely useful for documents created in applications without the Adobe PDF menu options and buttons.

Creating PDF documents is easy with Adobe Acrobat 8 Professional because it is a powerful and flexible software.

3

Combining Files

One of the terrific features of Adobe Acrobat 8 Professional is it allows you to combine different files into either a single PDF document or a PDF package. You can assemble files that are created from different applications. For example, you can combine a Word document, an Excel worksheet, and a PowerPoint slide into a single PDF document.

What is a PDF package? Consider a PDF package as a file folder that contains several PDF documents. When you open a PDF package in Adobe Acrobat Reader or Adobe Acrobat 8 Professional, you can view the list of documents in the same package and then you can select and view each document.

Acrobat Professional 8 offers a lot of flexibility and control to modify your pages after your PDF file has been created. You can insert, delete, replace, and rotate pages within your document.

Think of a PDF document as a designer dress. You acquired pieces of fabrics from different sources: Word, Excel, AutoCAD, and many others. Then you cut and sew them together using Acrobat Professional 8. To make the dress more appealing, you want to add some final elements—a few elegant buttons, for example. These elements come in form of header, footer, watermark, and background for your PDF document. They allow you to create PDF documents that have consistent and professional appearances.

Combining Files

The capability of combining files into a single PDF document is amazingly simple with Acrobat Professional 8. Once you have opened Acrobat Professional 8, you can use the **Combine Files...** button as shown in Figure 3-1 or go to the **File →** **Combine Files...** menu option to combine files.

Figure 3-1

The combine files wizard allows you to browse and select files you want to combine. You can move the order of the files by using Move Up or Move Down button. You can also remove files. Depending on your requirement, you can choose smaller files size with lower quality or larger files size with better quality.

Figure 3-2

In addition, you can choose pages within a document to be included in your final output. When you click on the **Choose Pages** button, you will see the "Preview and Select Page Range" screen that gives you the opportunity preview the actual document and to specify page range.

Figure 3-3

When you have finished your selections and settings, you can click on the **Create** button to produce your PDF document or PDF package.

Figure 3-4

You should view the "progress" screen to see the status of combining your files.

Figure 3-5

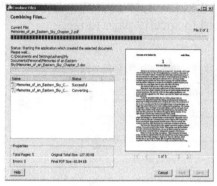

Once your files have been combined, you can choose the file location to name and save your file.

Figure 3-6

Modifying Pages

Users often need to modify pages within a PDF document. Acrobat Professional 8 contains many possible scenarios you would like to modify your pages including insert new pages, delete pages, replace pages, and rotate pages.

Inserting Pages

To add more pages to your document, you can go to **Document → Insert Pages...** or use shortcut keys [**Shift + Ctrl + I**]. First, you need to select the source document containing the pages you want to insert. Second, you should specify the location of where you want to insert these pages. For example, you can insert pages before the first page or after the last page.

Figure 3-7

Deleting Pages

You can delete pages from your PDF document by going to **Document → Delete Pages...** or using the shortcut keys [**Shift + Ctrl +D**]. You can either delete selected pages or enter the page range you want to delete.

Figure 3-8

Once you click on the **OK** button, you will be prompted with a warning message to confirm your deletion.

Replacing Pages

To replace pages in your PDF document, you can go to **Document → Replace Pages...** to select the document with your replacement pages in it. Once your document has been selected, you can specify the page range for replacement. You will see two sections: original and replacement files. You should indicate the page range needing to be replaced in the original document, then enter the page range from your replacement document.

Figure 3-9

Rotating Pages

When you combine files from different sources, you may have to rotate some pages in your document. You can rotate clockwise or counterclockwise with 90 degrees, or you can rotate 180 degrees. With your PDF document opened, you can go to **Document → Rotate Pages**, or use shortcut keys [**Shift + Ctrl +R**]. You should then see the "Rotate Pages" window opens.

Figure 3-10

You can specify your page range for your rotation. Also, you can indicate if you want to rotate even and odd pages, or even pages only, or odd pages only. If you would like to rotate pages with a specific orientation, you can select landscape pages, portrait pages, or pages with any orientation.

Please note that if you would like to preview your pages before actually rotate them, you can go to **View → Rotate View**, and then select whether you want to rotating **Clockwise** or **Counterclockwise**. The shortcut keys for clockwise is [**Shift + Ctrl + Plus**] and for counterclockwise is [**Shift + Ctrl + Minus**]. When you "rotate view," the page is only temporarily rotated and the rotation will not be saved. Once you are comfortable with your rotation from "rotate view," you can perform page rotation and save your file.

Moving Pages

If your page thumbnails pane has not been opened, you can open it with a single click on the **Pages** icon. When you move your mouse over to the **Pages** icon, you should see text "Pages: Go to specific pages using thumbnail images."

Figure 3-11

To move a page to a new location, you can click on its thumbnail image. Once the thumbnail image is highlighted, drag the page to its desired location. Please note that Acrobat Professional 8 will automatically renumber your pages in the page thumbnail pane.

 You can select multiple pages at the same time inside the page thumbnails pane by hold down the **Ctrl** key and then click on the pages you want to select.

Copying Pages

With the page thumbnails pane opened, you can copy any page in your PDF document. To copy a page in Windows, use **Ctrl** and drag the page thumbnail image to its second location. In Mac OS, you can use **Option** and drag the page thumbnail image to its second location. As soon as you release your mouse button, you should see that your page has been copied.

Creating a PDF Package

As we mentioned earlier, a PDF package works like a file folder that contains multiple PDF files. When you want to deliver several PDF documents in one package, you can use Acrobat Professional 8 to create a PDF package. In this way, you maintain the integrity of each individual document and bundle these related documents into one package. To create a PDF package, you can select the "Assemble Files into a PDF Package" option during the process of creating PDF document.

Figure 3-12

You can click on **Next** to continue.

Figure 3-13

You can view a screen showing you the progress of creating your PDF package.

Figure 3-14

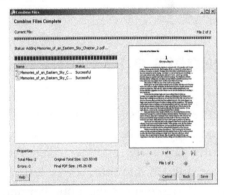

Once your PDF package has been produced, you can name it and save it into the location you desire. When you open your PDF package, you should see all individual PDF files inside your package. You can navigate these files and view them. If any of your PDF documents have digital signatures, your PDF package will maintain these properties and configuration settings.

Figure 3-15

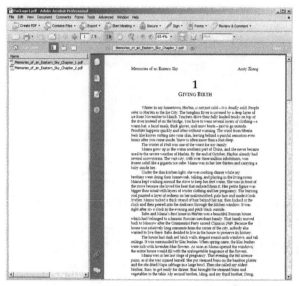

Adding Headers and Footers

You can add headers and footers into your combined PDF document. To add a header and/or a footer, you can go to **Document → Header & Footer**, and then select **Add**. Both header and footer are divided into three areas: left text, center text, and right text. You can insert a page number and date into any of these areas. Also, you can add custom text into any of these areas, then format your font in the font face and size that compliments the rest of your document.

Figure 3-16

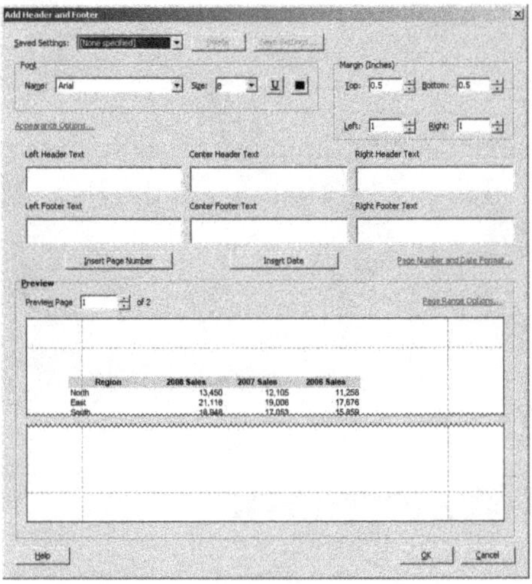

If you would like to save your current settings to use them again, just click on the **Save Settings** button.

Figure 3-17

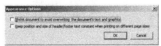

You can click on the **Appearance Options** hyperlink to select your document appearance settings, which include:

- shrinking document to avoid overwriting the document's text and graphics, and
- keeping the position and size of the header/footer text constant when printing on different page sizes.

Figure 3-18

You can also change the page number and date format to the style you desire.

Figure 3-19

In addition, you can specify the page range to apply to your custom header and footer by clicking on the **Page Range Options...** link.

Figure 3-20

Adding a Watermark

You can add a watermark to your PDF document by using **Document → Watermark,** then click on **Add.** You should see the **Add Watermark** screen with options for your watermark. You can either enter watermark text or use an external file. If you choose an external file, you can select the page number of the absolute scale of the text you want to place as the watermark. If you enter your custom text, you can format the font, size, color, and alignment. You can choose from three alignments: left, center, or right.

Figure 3-21

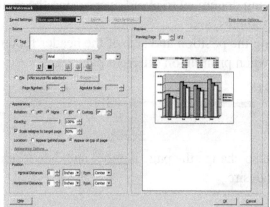

Watermark Appearance

The watermark appearance comes with four properties:
rotation, opacity, scale, and location. We will cover all these
attributes in this section.

You choose the rotation of your watermark text from four
options: none, 45 degrees (45°), minus 45 degrees (-45°), or a
custom degree.

Opacity means the degree you can see through an object or
text. When you set opacity to 100, your watermark will have its
fullest visibility.

The scale, relative to your document page, determines your
watermark size within your document. By default, this value
sets at 50%.

Figure 3-22

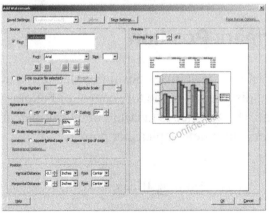

The location setting for your watermark text or object is
also crucial to its overall appearance. You can choose either
"appear behind the page" or "appear in front of the page." The
difference between these two options are not obvious when you
are working with a document full of text. But when you work

with documents using graphics or other objects, the difference is very obvious. If you set your watermark to appear in front of the page, then it will always appear on top of the other document elements including text and graphics as shown in Figure 3-22. When you set your watermark to appear behind the page, your watermark will be covered by graphic elements as shown in Figure 3-23.

Figure 3-23

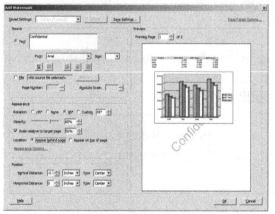

Watermark Position

You can set your watermark position based on vertical or horizontal distance from the top, center, or bottom of your document. The distance is measure in inches, percent, centimeters, millimeters, picas, or points.

Inches, Picas, and Points

If you have worked with typesetting or publication design, picas and points are your friends in various applications such as QuarkXPress, PageMaker, or InDesign. If you are not familiar with picas and points, then here is a quick overview. It is not very easy to divide your document into tiny spaces with inches. For example, if you use a standard sheet of paper, 8.5 by 11 inches, and try to create a brochure in three folds, then you get approximately 3.6667 inches per fold. That is not easy to measure. Using picas and points makes layouts much easier. Each inch equals 6 picas so there are 66 picas for 11 inches. For the same three-fold brochure, you have 22 picas per fold, which is much easier to understand and work with. Therefore, you can use picas to measure relatively larger spaces such as column width, length, and margins.

A point is the smallest measurement unit that is usually used for fonts. One pica contains 12 points. Therefore, 5 points can be represented as 0**p**5—meaning zero pica with five points and 17 points will be represented as 1**p**5 since one pica contains 12 points. Please note that the letter **p** represents pica.

With all these different units of measurements, you should be able to place your watermark anywhere on the document with precision.

Adding Background Colors or Images

You can present your PDF document with a consistent feel and look, by adding a background color or image to it. To add a background color or image, you can use **Document →Background**, and then click on the **Add/Replace** option. You can choose the source for a background color, or use an image file as your background. Similar to a watermark, you can define the appearance and position of your background.

Figure 3-24

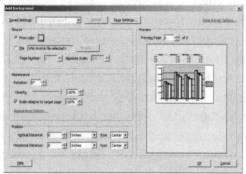

Summary

You can combine files that are created from different applications into a single PDF document. When you combine files together, you can also specify the pages you want to include instead of an entire file. Also, you can combine files into a PDF package that contains individual PDF files. This is a new feature in Adobe Acrobat 8 Professional. The PDF package you create is similar to a file folder that maintains the integrity of the individual files.

Inside your PDF document, you can modify pages within your document with easy-to-use menu options and a page thumbnails pane to insert pages, delete pages, replace pages, rotate pages, move pages, and copy pages.

Adobe Acrobat 8 Professional gives you a lot tools to create a coherent, professional-looking document. In the latter part of this chapter, we covered how to add headers, footers, watermarks, and background. You can use header and footer to place document titles, page numbers, or renumber your pages, and include special touches to your document with watermarks, background color, or images.

4

Exporting Documents

Without the capability of exporting a PDF document into other document formats, Acrobat Professional 8 would work like a one-way street—a telephone without a speaker or a vehicle without reverse. This is because exporting documents is an essential function that allow you to convert PDF documents into the file format that your user needs. For example, a PDF document with a list of prescription drugs can be exported into an XML format and allow other systems to utilize the same list without duplicating the data-entry efforts.

Since not everybody has Acrobat Professional 8, another important aspect of exporting PDF documents is allowing users to edit a portion or the entire document in other applications such as Microsoft Word. You can export your PDF document, whether it is a chart, table, image, or a block of text, then empower other users to modify, convert, copy, or distribute from various applications.

This chapter describes the process of exporting PDF documents into other file formats.

Export Menu

You can export documents from a PDF into other formats such as Word, XML, Rich Text, Post Script, HTML, image files, and plain text using the **Export** button.

Figure 4-1

Also, you can use **File → Export**, then select the file format you want to export: Word, Rich Text, XML 1.0, HTML, image, text, PostScript, PDF/A, and PDF/X.

Figure 4-2

Exporting PDF Document to Word

When you export PDF document into Microsoft Word, the page layout and table structure should be converted into proper Word format. This is a very useful feature for users need to perform an edit on the PDF file in Word. To export your PDF document into Word, simply select Word from the export menu.

Please note that if your PDF document contains objects from applications such as Excel and Project, these objects will not be editable in the Word document you have exported.

Another observation while exporting PDF document into Word is—paragraphs are usually converted into text blocks within a text box.

Figure 4-3

> **Create PDF Document**
> **from PDF Printer|**

 The best candidate for export into a Word document is a PDF document created from Word initially. I have experienced issues with a PDF document created from various sources such as text boxes overlapping as shown in Figure 4-4.

Figure 4-4

> The weather worsenfile looked
> by the minute but Balback again
> hard not come home that would

Exporting PDF Document to HTML or XML

If you need to display your document on a web page, you can export your PDF document into an HTML format. You can also export your document into an XML 1.0 format. Because XML is widely used in web sites, web services, and many other technologies, your document can be used for data interchange, transmission, processing, and display. XML 1.0 became a

World Wide Web Consortium (W3C) recommendation since 1998 and it became a simple, standard, and elegant data structure.

To export into an HTML or XML document, you can use the **Export** button or use **File → Export**, then select either the HTML or XML document type.

Figure 4-5

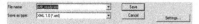

You can click on the **Settings…** button to modify and save document settings such as encoding options, bookmarks, and image file settings.

Figure 4-6

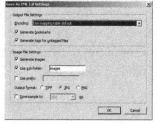

Exporting PDF Document to Text

There are two types of text documents: Rich Text and plain text. Rich Text (RTF) format supports text formatting, colors, alignment, bullets, and links. To export into a RTF and plain text document, you can use the **Export** button or use **File → Export**, then select Rich Text, Text (Accessible), or Text (plain).

Before you create your Rich Text document, you can click on the **Settings…** button to change document settings such as the comments settings or image settings.

Figure 4-7

Before you export it as a plain text document, you can click on the **Settings...** button to change the document settings such as the Output File Settings or Image File Settings.

Figure 4-8

You may notice that when you try to export an accessible text document, the **Settings...** button is disabled because links and images are not available for accessibility reasons.

Exporting a PDF Document to Images

There are two options for exporting your PDF document into images: exporting the entire document into image(s) or exporting each image within your PDF document into an image file format. In this section, we are going to explore both options.

Exporting the Entire PDF Document into Image(s)

With your PDF document opened inside Acrobat Professional 8, you can use **File → Export → Image**, and then select one of the following image formats: JPEG, JPEG2000, PNG, or TIFF. Alternatively, you can use the **Export** button and select your image format.

Image Types

When you create, share, and archive images, you have to consider two major factors: image size and picture quality. Better picture quality usually means a bigger file size. With limited storage space, you have to perform trade-off analysis for your image files.

There are many image formats available and each format has its own characteristics. Images can be compressed to make the file size smaller than its original file. They can also be uncompressed. There are two types of compressions: lossy and lossless. A lossy compression usually produces a smaller file size than a lossless compression because it discards part of the image data. So a lossy compressed image has a smaller size and lower quality.

JPEG means "Joint Photographic Expert Group" and it employs lossy compression. This image format is frequently used in digital cameras and web sites. It retains image details that matter most to the human eye. For example, we are more likely to notice changes in brightness than the changes in colors.

TIFF means "Tagged Image File Format" and it can be uncompressed or compressed with a lossless compression. TIFF images are popular in the publishing industry because they can store multiple layers of images and each channel has 16 bits in depth—doubled the standard 8 bits per channel. TIFF images are larger than the same image stored as a JPEG.

PNG means "Portable Network Graphics" and it is similar to TIFF in terms of image quality and channel depth. PNG images support lossless compression and it incorporates preprocessing filters to improve compression efficiency. PNG images and TIFF images are ideal for archive purposes.

If your PDF document has multiple pages, each page will be exported into an individual image file.

Exporting Each Image within a PDF Document

To export every image within your PDF document, you can use **Advanced → Document Processing → Export All Images...** to start the process.

Figure 4-9

You will be prompted to select image types and file names when you want to export. If you have several images in your document, Acrobat Professional 8 will automatically add suffixes after your file name, including the page number and image number. For example, if you entered "main_text" as a file name and there are three images on page 4, the first image is "main_text_Page_4_Image_0001.jpg" as its file name.

Figure 4-10

If you click on **Settings…** button, you can further refine your export criteria in these categories: file settings, color management, conversion, and extraction. File settings include grayscale, color, and format. Color management includes RGB, CMYK, Grayscale, and Other. Conversion includes colorspace and resolution. These settings are essential for your image quality and image size, the higher the quality, the larger the size. You can also exclude images that are smaller than a specified size, for example, less than 1 inch.

Figure 4-11

Once you are ready, you can click on the OK button to start your export process.

 Please note that you cannot export vector objects, only raster images.

Raster Images and Vector Objects

Raster images are created from scanning artwork from a scanner or "painting" inside applications such as Adobe PhotoShop, Macromedia Fireworks, or Corel Paint. These images are composed of a collection of dots—also called pixels. Each pixel is a very small, colored square unit for your image. After scanning your artwork, your scanner converted your artwork into a collection of pixels. When you are taking pictures from your digital camera, "painting" your images in PhotoShop, or printing your images from your printer, their resolutions are measured in dots per inch, or dpi. Most images for print production should have 300 pixels-per-inch resolution or higher. When you scale up or down raster images, you may notice the loss of image quality.

Vector objects, on the other hand, do not suffer loss of image quality when you change their scales. Vector images are based on lines and curves that connected to each other to produce graphical objects. These lines and curves are based on graphical nodes that are calculated mathematically. You can create vector images from various applications such as Adobe Illustrator, Macromedia Freehand, or CorelDRAW. When you change your vector image scale, the lines and curves are scaled accordingly and you can output your vector image into any resolution. So vector images are ideal for clip art or company logos.

Summary

In this chapter, we covered how to export PDF documents into other document formats. When a user wants to edit, copy, share, or archive documents in other applications, you can operate this feature to export your PDF documents.

First, we discussed how to export a PDF document into Word. Second, we described how to export a PDF document into an HTML or XML format. HTML and XML documents have a wide range of uses, including web sites and web services. Then, we covered how to export a PDF document into rich text or plain text documents. Finally, we introduced exporting PDF documents into image files. There are two ways of exporting PDF documents into image files: exporting the entire PDF document into image(s) and exporting each image within a PDF document.

5

Review and Comment

We start this chapter by introducing reviews: e-mail reviews and shared reviews. E-mail reviews are ideal for reviewers are that scattered in different geographic locations and do not always have access to a common server location. Shared reviews are more suited for reviewers working behind a firewall who have access to a network share folder. Reviewers participating in the shared reviews receive notifications whenever new comments are published once they have opened their PDF document.

Adobe Acrobat 8 Professional offers a wide range of tools for reviewers to use to provide comment and markups on PDF documents. These tools include sticky notes, callout, textbox, text edits, stamps, highlights, cloud, and various shapes. We will also cover how to set comment preferences and how to record an audio comment. With so many tools available, reviewers should be able to provide comments and markups with professional efficiency as well as gracefulness.

Publishing comments or adding markups are easy to accomplish. We will discuss how to publish a comment, add a markup, or publish a comment from other reviewers who do not have access to the comment server. You can also attach an external comment to your document, reply to a comment, or set comment status. The comment navigation pane is very useful since it contains many comment-related functions all in a centralized area. These functions include search and filter comments, a print comment summary, setting status and checkmark, and sort comments. We will also introduce you to how to delete a comment, check spelling, and import and export comments.

In the last section of this chapter, we will discuss how to start a meeting utilizing Adobe Connect. You will find information about how to: start a meeting, invite meeting attendees, share your computer screen, and how to join a meeting. Conducting meeting can be a useful way to communicate with all reviewers.

Reviews

Creating an E-mail Review

Anybody can participate in an e-mail based review as long as he/she has Adobe Reader 7 and above or Adobe Acrobat 6 and above. Reviewers will receive appropriate tools and instruction for posting their reviews and then they will submit their reviews to you through e-mail. Once you have received their reviews, you can merge all the reviews, consolidating them into your PDF document.

 How to Enable Commenting in Adobe Reader
Reviewers can enable commenting in Adobe Reader by following these steps: 1) open the PDF document in Adobe Reader; 2) Go to **Comments → Enable For Commenting** to enable the commenting functions in Adobe Reader; 3) save this PDF document.

To create an e-mail review, you can go to **Comments →
Attach for E-mail Review** or use the **Review & Comment**
button then select **Attach for E-mail Review**.

Figure 5-1

If this is the first time you have used this feature, you have to
set up your e-mail review profile including your name, title,
company, and e-mail address.

Figure 5-2

Once you have completed your profile entry, you will be in
step 1 of 3: Initiating an E-mail Based Review. This screen
introduces the e-mail review process.

Figure 5-3

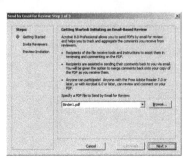

During step 2 of 3: Invite Reviewers, you can select your designated reviewers from your company's e-mail address book or type the e-mail addresses manually into the textbox.

Figure 5-4

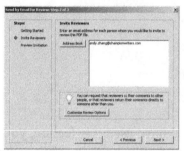

If you click on the **Customize Review Options** button, you are prompted with review options. By default, users can post their reviews if they have free Adobe Reader 7 or above. You can disable this option here by deselecting the checkbox.

Figure 5-5

At step 3 of 3: Preview Invitation, you can review the default invitation message and make changes if needed.

Figure 5-6

Once you click on the **Send Invitation** button, you will be prompted with an alert box with messages about your e-mail application's behavior for sending invitations. Most e-mail applications will send out invitations automatically, including Outlook. If your e-mail application does not send out invitations automatically, you have to send out invitations manually. You can disable this alert box so it will not show up the next time by selecting the checkbox.

Figure 5-7

Your reviewers should receive your invitations soon through e-mail. A typical invitation has your invitation message with your PDF document as an attachment.

Figure 5-8

Sending for Shared Review

Shared review is ideal for reviewers who have access to a common network server and work behind a firewall. Shared reviews are published to a shared comment folder for all reviewers to access. With shared reviews, reviewers receive notice on all new comments since the last time they opened the document. When reviewers open their PDF document, all comments are synchronized between the local version and the server version.

When you want to send your PDF document for shared review, you can use **Comments → Send for Shared Review** or use the **Review & Comment** button, then select **Send for Shared Review**. Please note that all reviewers (including yourself) should have write access privileges to your shared comment folder.

Selecting Shared Location

If you have not designated a shared comment folder on your network, then you need to add a new shared comment folder by clicking on the **Add New Location...** button. Otherwise, you can select your shared comment folder.

Figure 5-9

To add a shared comment folder, you should give your comment folder a name that is easy to understand and remember. Then, you can select what type of comment folder it should be from one of these three options: Network Folder, SharePoint workspace, or WebDAV server. Then click on **Next** to continue.

Figure 5-10

During this Configure Location step, you can browse to your network folder or enter your folder name manually, according to the instructions. You can click on the **Verify** button to make sure your comment folder path is valid. Your comment folder will be added once you click on the **Add Folder** button.

Figure 5-11

With your comment folder selected, you can click on the **Next** button to continue.

Figure 5-12

Selecting Send Options

You can now determine how your PDF document will be sent: either by automatically sending the document to your reviewers, or saving the file locally. Also, if you choose to automatically send the document to your reviewers, you can decide whether to attach your document and save a local copy, or just send the document link. You can click the **Next** button to continue.

Figure 5-13

Select Your Preferred E-mail Applications

If a user has more than one e-mail application installed on his/her computer, the user can set the preferred e-mail applications for sending comments.

In Windows, a user can go to Control Panel, then open **Internet Options**. Once inside the Internet Properties window, navigate to the **Programs** tab. You can select your preferred e-mail program. Please note that users must restart Acrobat Professional 8 in order for the changes to take effect.

In Mac OS, a user can go to **Mail → Preferences** and select **General**. From the default e-mail reader menu, a user can select a preferred e-mail application. Please note that users must restart Acrobat Professional 8 in order for the changes to take effect.

Inviting Reviewers

There are two groups of reviewers you can invite: required reviewers and optional reviewers. If you have more than one e-mail address, you can separate them with either a semicolon or press enter key to add the new e-mail address as a new line. During this step you can also set a deadline for comment. Click on the **Next** button to continue.

Figure 5-14

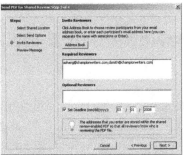

Previewing Your Message

You can review and edit your review message subject and body text before you submit your message during this step. Click on the **Finish** button to complete the process.

Figure 5-15

If your e-mail application is properly configured, you should then see a confirmation message.

Figure 5-16

Adding New Reviewers or E-mailing All Reviewers

If you forgot to include some reviewers in your initial invitation, you can add more reviewers later. To add more reviewers, you can go to the **Comments → Review Tracker** or use the **Review & Comment** button, and then select **Review Tracker**.

In the Review Tracker window, you should be able to see a list of reviews you have sent, reviews you have joined, and review servers. With the review document selected, you should be able to **E-mail All Reviewers** or **Add New Reviewers**.

Figure 5-17

Review Tracker

Review tracker helps you manage your reviews. From the Review Tracker window, you can examine reviews you have sent and reviews you have joined.

Figure 5-18

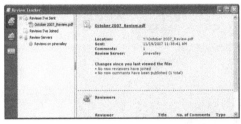

You can also rejoin reviews, navigate to review servers, click on the document hyperlink to open a document, or access e-mail properties (including e-mail addresses and user names). In addition, you can use the Review Tracker window to manage the form and subscribe to RSS ("Really Simple Syndication") feeds.

Figure 5-19

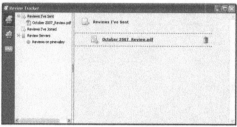

Saving an Archive Copy

If you want to save a copy of your PDF document along with all reviews, you can save an archive copy by going to **File →** **Save as Archive Copy** for shared reviews or **File → Save As...** to save your archived copy. Your archived copy will contain the document content and all existing comments. This copy is disconnected from the shared review server so you can edit both the document content and comments.

Figure 5-20

For a browser-based review, you can use **Comments → Work Offline** to disconnect from the comment server. Once you have disconnected from the comment server, you will see that a new ribbon is added to your document menu area, which you can use to reconnect to your review server.

Figure 5-21

You can also click on the **Check Server Status** button (on the right) to check your review server status.

Opening the Shared Review

When you are ready to open the shared review, you can click on the PDF document link. You should see a Welcome Back to Shared Review screen with reviewers and comments information. You will find all the latest reviews since the last time you opened your document.

Figure 5-22

Comment and Markup Tools

Setting Comment Preferences

You can configure your comment preferences by going to **Edit → Preferences...** or using the shortcut keys [**Ctrl + K**] to open the Preferences screen. From the commenting category, you can change numerous comment preferences such as font, font size, pup-up opacity, pop-up open behavior, and making comments.

Figure 5-23

The Comment & Markup toolbar contains many devices you can use for adding your comments or markups to a PDF document. If you don't see the Comments & Markup toolbar, you can go to **View → Toolbars**, then select **Comment & Markup** to open it.

Figure 5-24

Adding a Sticky Note

You can place a sticky note to a PDF document to share your notes or comments. To add a sticky note, use the Sticky Note tool from the Comment & Markup toolbar, or go to **Comments → Add Sticky Note**, or use the shortcut keys [**Ctrl + 6**]. You can move your sticky note anywhere in the document by dragging the sticky note placement anchor to your desired location. Please note that spell check is enabled by default for sticky notes. Your sticky note is automatically tagged with your name, and date and time information.

Figure 5-25

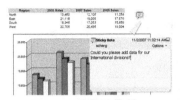

After you have completed your message inside the pop-up note, you can click elsewhere in the document and the note text will then be hidden. When you mouse over the note anchor, the note text will be visible again.

Figure 5-26

You can access to other Sticky Note properties by clicking on **Options** to open the Options menu at the upper right hand corner of the pop-up note. Sticky Note properties include: set status, show comments list, and reply.

Figure 5-27

You can set status for your sticky note. Here is the list of possible status:

Table 5-1

Migration:
None
Not Confirmed
Confirmed
Review:
None
Accepted
Cancelled
Completed
Rejected

Text Edits

You can use the Text Edits tool from the Comment & Markup toolbar to perform text edit markups such as insert, delete, or replace text contents. The Text Edits tool works like a copy editors' pen. When you use the Text Edits tool for the first time, you should see an information screen for Text Edits tool.

Figure 5-28

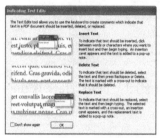

Inserting Text

To insert text, you can click on the Text Edits tool to enable it and place your cursor at the position where you would like to insert your text, then type your text. You should see an insert mark with your text inside your PDF document.

Figure 5-29

Deleting Text

With the Text Edits tool enabled, you can select the text you want to delete, then press the **Delete** or **Backspace** key. As soon as you press the **Delete** or **Backspace** key, you should see that the text is crossed out.

Figure 5-30

over ~~cold~~ melon

Replacing Text

Replacing text is a combination of delete and insert—you delete the original text and insert the replacement text. To replace text, you can select the text portion you want to delete then start typing replacement text. You should see the original text is then marked for deletion and the replacement text is now marked for insertion.

Figure 5-31

Stamp Tool

The stamp tool allows you to add a stamp into your PDF document. Stamps are grouped into three categories: dynamic, sign here, or standard business.

Dynamic Stamps

You can add dynamic stamps into your PDF documents such as revised, reviewed, received, approved, and confidential. Dynamic stamps will tag the date and time, along with your user name, inside the stamp.

Figure 5-32

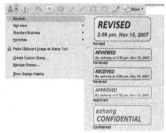

Sign Here

Just like its name indicates, Sign Here stamps give you the popular options to prompt users to sign the document at specified places. The Sign Here stamps include: Witness, Initial Here, Sign Here, Accepted, and Rejected.

Figure 5-33

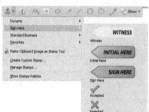

Standard Business

Standard Business stamps include a large collection of frequently used stamps such as Approved, Not Approved, Draft, Final, Completed, and many others.

Figure 5-34

Other Stamp Options

If you use a few stamps frequently, you can add them to your Favorites list and they will show up on top of the stamp menu. To add a stamp to your Favorites list, you can place your stamp anywhere in your document, then click on the stamp to select it. You will then see a set of handles tagged to your selected stamp. After you've selected your stamp, go to **Favorites →
Add Current Stamp To Favorites** to add your stamp to your Favorites list.

Figure 5-35

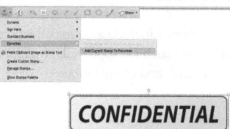

Even though there are so many stamps to choose from, you may still want to create your own custom stamp. To create a custom stamp, go to **Create Custom Stamp...** and select your file.

Highlighting Text

If you want to highlight a section of text in your document, you can use the select text tool.

Figure 5-36

With your select text tool active, you can drag over the text and the selected text will be highlighted in yellow. This tool works like a highlighter.

Figure 5-37

Rigatoni Alla Coupe ....
rigatoni with italian sausage, mushrooms, tomato and cream

Underline and Cross Out Text Tool

You can use the underline text tool to underline your selected text. The cross out text tool allows you to cross out your selected text.

Figure 5-38

Callout Tool

You can use the text callout tool to create a callout arrow and a text comment area. You can change the shape of callout arrow by selecting it, then using its handles to modify the shape.

Figure 5-39

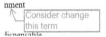

Textbox Tool

The standard textbox tool is very similar to the callout tool except it does not have the callout arrow.

Figure 5-40

Cloud Tool

You can use the cloud tool to draw a cloud in the document, then provide comments in the comment box.

Figure 5-41

Other Shapes

You can draw other shapes in your PDF document using the arrow, line, rectangle, oval, polygon line, polygon, and pencil tools.

Figure 5-42

Group and Ungroup Markups

When you want to group several markup elements together, you can use select (or hand) tool to select a markup, then use **Ctrl** key plus mouse click when using Windows or **Command** key plus mouse click when using Mac OS to select all other markups. When you right click on your selected markups, you can choose the **Group** option from the pop-up menu to group them together.

To ungroup your markups, you can right click with your mouse, or use **Ctrl** plus mouse click on the grouped area and choose **Ungroup** from the pop-up menu to dissolve your grouped markup elements.

Showing Comments on a Page

If you are wondering how a comment would look on the page, you can select comment and then select the **Show** button from the Comment & Markup toolbar.

Figure 5-43

Record Audio Comment

You can record an audio comment into your PDF document along with your text document. To record an audio comment, you can click on the Record Audio Comment tool from the Comment & Markup toolbar.

Figure 5-44

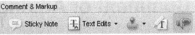

 If you don't see this Record Audio Comment tool, you can go to **Tools → Customize Toolbars...** and open the More Tools screen. If you select the Record Audio Comment checkbox and click on OK, the Record Audio Comment tool will show up in your Comment & Markup toolbar.

Figure 5-45

After you have clicked on the Record Audio Comment tool from the Comment & Markup toolbar, you can anchor your audio comment to the position you want. Locate your desired position inside the PDF document, click when you reach it, then a Sound Recorder will show up to allow you to record your sound file.

Figure 5-46

Comments

Publishing a Comment or Adding a Markup

When you are ready to provide a comment or add a markup to a PDF document, you can either click on the attachment or go to the URL to locate this document. With your PDF document opened, you may need to confirm that you are going to join the share review. Then you can use Comments & Markup tools to add your input. Once you have added your comment to a PDF document, you will be asked if you want to publish it.

Figure 5-47

Once you have published your review, it will save your review to a shared comment folder. When other reviewers open the document, they will see an alert box indicating a new comment has been published. Other reviewers have the option to open and view this comment.

Figure 5-48

Publishing Comments from Others

If a reviewer cannot access to your comment server, you can publish comments on behalf of that reviewer. If that reviewer has completed the comment inside the PDF document, then you can use **Comments → Import Comments...** to select and import comments from a different reviewer.

Attaching a Comment

All comment tools are ideal for brief comments. When your comment is too large to fit inside the PDF document, you should consider attaching your comment with your document. To attach your comment file, you can click on the Attach a File as Comment tool from the Comment & Markup toolbar. If you don't see the Attach a File as Comment tool in the Comment & Markup toolbar, you can go to **Tools → Customize Toolbars...** to open the More Tools screen. If you select the Attach a File as Comment checkbox and then click on OK, the Attach a File as Comment tool will show up in your Comment & Markup toolbar.

Figure 5-49

As soon as you click on the Attach a File as Comment tool, your cursor will turn into an attachment pin. You can use the attachment pin to position your comment. Once you have anchored your comment inside your PDF document, you can then select your comment file, and you should see a paper clip icon for your comment attachment file.

Figure 5-50

Please note the difference between Attach a File as Comment file and attach a document file. When you attach a comment file, your comment is integrated into your comment workflow, and it will be viewable for eligible reviewers. When you attach a document from the **Document → Attach a File...**, or use the **Attach a File** (paperclip) icon, the file you attach is associated with your PDF document as an attachment, not a comment.

Figure 5-51

Replying to a Comment

You can right click on a comment and select **Reply** to respond to a comment. When multiple reviewers reply to the same comment, these replies will group into a single thread.

Setting Comment Status and Checkmark

Comment status and checkmark can help you to review all comments quickly if your PDF document contains a lot of comments. It can also help all reviewers to know the status of comments. You can either right click on the comment then select Set Comment Status from the pop-up menu, or click the Set Status button.

Figure 5-52

To set a checkmark, you can either right click on the comment then select checkmark from the pop-up menu, or click the **Checkmark** button. You can also place a checkmark for a comment by clicking on the checkbox in front of a comment inside the comment navigation pane.

Figure 5-53

Printing Comment Summary

With Acrobat Professional 8, you can print your PDF document along with a summary of comments by using **Comments →
Print With Comments Summary**, or use shortcut keys [**Ctrl + T**]. You should see the Summarize Options screen with four print layout options: 1) document and comments with connector lines on separate page; 2) document and comments with connector lines on single pages; 3) comments only; or 4) document and comments with sequence numbers. You can also choose font size, connector line color, and other properties.

Figure 5-54

Filtering Comments

If you want to print only selected comments, you can use filter options by clicking the **Show** button. You can filter by type, reviewer, status, and checked date. You can also click the **Sort** button to select comments by type, page, author, date, color, checkmark status, and status by person.

Figure 5-55

Searching Comments

With the comment navigation pane open, you can click on the **Search** button to look for comments with your search text.

Figure 5-56

You should be able to search comments from the search screen. You can also indicate if you want to search whole words only or case-sensitive.

Figure 5-57

Deleting Comment

When you want to delete a comment, you can Right-click on the comment in Windows, or Control-click on the comment in Mac OS, and choose the Delete option from the pop-up menu. You can also delete your comment by clicking the **Delete** button (Trash Can icon) from the comment navigation pane when your comment is selected.

Figure 5-58

Checking Comment Spelling

You can perform spell check on your comments by going to **Edit → Check Spelling**, then select **In Comments...**, or use shortcut key [**F7**]. During your spell checking, you can click on **Change** to accept the suggestion or click the **Undo Edit** to reverse your changes.

Figure 5-59

Importing Comments

In this section, we are going to cover how to import and export comments. You can import comments from either a PDF document, or a Form Data Format (FDF) file, or XML-based Form Data Format (XFDF) file. To import comments, go to the **Comments → Import Comments...**, and then select your comment file.

Figure 5-60

Exporting Comments

When you are ready to export comments, go to **Comments** then choose **Export Comments to Word...**, or **Export Comments to AutoCAD...**, or the **Export Comments to Data File...** option. If you choose to export to data file, you can choose either FDF file, or XFDF file.

Meetings

Starting a Meeting

You can start a meeting using Adobe Acrobat Connect. To start a meeting, you can use **File → Start Meeting...** or click on the **Start Meeting** button. If you already have an Adobe Acrobat

Connect account, then you can go ahead and log into your meeting portal. Otherwise, you can create a trial account and test out the features during the trial period.

Figure 5-61

You can specify a unique URL for your meetings.

Figure 5-62

Once your URL has been accepted, you can click the **Start Meeting** button to begin your meeting. Please note that you will need Flash Player version 8.0.22, or above, for your browser for your meeting. If your browser does not have Flash Player 8.0.22 or above installed, you should see a message similar to this:

Flash Player 8.0.22.0 or above is required

Adobe Acrobat Connect requires the Flash Player browser plug-in, version 8.0.22.0 or above. Please download and install the Flash Player to continue.

Download Flash Player

You can click on the download link to download and install Flash Player.

Once you log into your meeting portal, you should see your welcome screen. You can click on **Send an E-mail Invitation** button to invite people to your meeting or click on **Share My Screen** button to start sharing your screen.

Figure 5-63

Inviting Meeting Attendees

As soon as you click on Send An E-mail Invitation button, your E-mail application should start with a new message with default meeting invitation inside the E-mail body text. You can enter your recipient's E-mail address and send your invitation.

Figure 5-64

When meeting attendees received your E-mail, they can attend your meeting according to your meeting instruction including phone conference number.

Sharing Screen

To share your screen, you must have the Adobe Connect add-in component installed. If you don't have this component installed, then you will be prompted with for installation when you use this feature for the first time. After clicking on the **Share My Screen** button, you can decide what screen area you want to share: Desktop, Windows, or Applications.

Figure 5-64

When you select sharing Desktop, you will be broadcasting your entire computer screen. If you select Windows, then you will have to choose which window you want to share, and your screen will only broadcast to the users from this window. Other active windows will not be broadcast to meeting attendees. If you select Applications, every action you take in that application will be shared to your meeting attendees.

To stop sharing, you can simply click on the **Stop Sharing** button when you are in the shared screen, window, or application. The **Stop Sharing** button is typically located on the top of the active screen, window, or application.

Figure 5-65

Stop Sharing

Joining a Meeting

When meeting attendees join a meeting, they can see several panes on the left side: Camera, Attendee List, Chat, and Note. You will view all meeting attendees in the Attendee List. You can chat with all meeting attendees, the presenter, or any individual attendee by enter your message into the chat pod. After you have selected your target audience, you can send your chat message. You can also take notes from your meeting inside the note pod. In addition, you can change your text size, alignment, or e-mail your note from the note pane.

Figure 5-66

Often times during the meeting, you may want to allow other meeting attendees to be able to share their screen. As a meeting host, you can click on the meeting attendee's name, then change the setting for that meeting attendee into a presenter. Once a meeting attendee becomes a presenter, he or she can share his screen to all meeting attendees.

Summary

This is a chapter focused on the feedback and communications of document reviewers. After you have created your PDF document, you may need to share it with other reviewers and solicit their comments. We covered three important aspects of Adobe Acrobat 8 Professional: reviews, comments, and meetings.

There are two types of reviews: e-mail review and shared review. Everybody who has Adobe Reader 7 and above or Adobe Acrobat 6 and above can conduct e-mail reviews. If your reviewers are on the same network and they have access to your comment server, then you can consider shared review. In this chapter, we covered how to use review tracker, add new reviewers, and a few other functions related to reviews.

Adobe Acrobat 8 Professional contains many comment and markup tools. In this chapter, we introduced these tools and how to add comments or markups to your document. You can print, filter, sort, set status, and search your comments inside the comment navigation pane. We also discussed how to import and export comments.

This chapter is not complete without showing you how to conduct meetings because once all reviewers have reviewed and commented on the PDF document, they may request to have a meeting. With Adobe Connect, you can start a meeting, invite attendees, and share your screen. Meeting attendees can send questions and write their own notes, all while seeing your shared screen and your document.

6

Basic Forms

We have to fill out forms on various occasions: signing up
for a class, applying for a new job or purchasing a new home.
Paper forms usually require two processes: providing the
form information and entering the form data into a system.
Oftentimes, users fill out the fields on paper forms and
someone else enters the data. This is not the most efficient way
of processing user data and it is prone to error.

The interactive PDF forms we are going to discuss in
this chapter allow users to provide data directly into the
interactive form, and then submit the form via the Internet
or through a Local Area Network. The receiver of the forms
can automatically collect the data submitted by users. This
eliminates the need for second data entry and streamlines
the process. There are also other security features that can be
applied to interactive forms to ensure a user's authenticity and
to protect sensitive data. There are two types of PDF forms:
fill-and-print forms and fill-and-submit forms. With fill-and-
print forms, users type their information into the forms and
then print the forms. They can hand-deliver, mail or fax the
forms. User data within fill-and-submit forms can be submitted
directly via email or online.

Converting to interactive PDF forms is also an easy process.

You can convert your Adobe InDesign layout, Excel spreadsheet or Word document into interactive PDF forms. You can also scan your paper form into interactive PDF forms.

Creating a New Form

There are several ways to create a new PDF form. If you already have a paper format form, you can use a scanner to convert your paper form into a PDF. You can also convert an existing form from other file formats into an interactive PDF form. To create a new form, you can go to **Forms → Create a New Form...** from the quick start menu.

Figure 6-1

You can also use **Forms → Create a New Form...** from the application menu.

Figure 6-2

At the "Create a New Form" screen, you have four options from which to create a new interactive form: select a template, start with an electronic document, import data from a spreadsheet and scan from paper.

Figure 6-3

The next screen (which can be disabled) will inform you that creating new forms or editing forms can be done through Adobe LiveCycle Designer. Adobe LiveCycle Designer is a powerful tool for creating interactive forms. This independent application comes with Adobe Acrobat 8 Professional.

Figure 6-4

As soon as you click on **"Continue"**, Adobe LiveCycle Designer will open. You have a wide range of commonly used form templates from which to choose, including Check Request, Expense Account and Invoice. You can add your company logo to these templates.

Figure 6-5

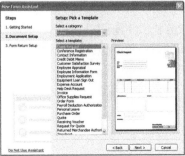

We use the conference registration form template as an example. During the document setup process, you can enter your company name, select your company logo, and add other information such as company address, phone, fax, conference name, date and location.

Figure 6-6

At the end of your form creation, you can add an email button and a print button to your form.

Figure 6-7

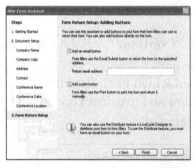

Once you have clicked on the "**Finish**" button, you should see your form open in design view inside Adobe LiveCycle Designer.

Figure 6-8

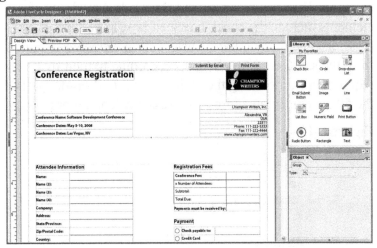

Because Adobe LiveCycle Designer has a lot of pre-built form elements from which to choose, you can simply use these elements on your form with little or no customization. You can create your form and preview it in PDF immediately from the "Preview PDF" navigation tab.

Figure 6-9

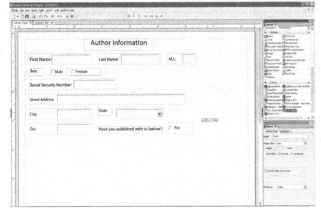

Adobe LiveCycle Designer 8 has three groups of form elements: Standard, Custom and Bar Code. Standard form elements include the check box, text box, radio button, drop-down list and many others. Custom form elements are derived from the standard form elements according to their own requirements, including the United States (a drop-down list of the 50 states), email address, address block and more.

Figure 6-10

Tooltip Property

To improve the accessibility of the form you have created, you can add the Tooltip property to the form elements, such as text box and drop-down list. When visually impaired or motion-challenged users open your form, they will be able to benefit from the Tooltip text and tags and will know the field description. To enable the Tooltip property, you can go to the Binding tab in your form element's properties window and then provide a meaningful description in the name field.

Figure 6-11

Enable Users to Save Form Data from Adobe Reader

When users open your form from Adobe Reader, they will not be able to save filled-in copies of your form unless you give them permission to do so. You can go to **Advanced → Enable Usage Rights in Adobe Reader...** to enable users to save form data from Adobe Reader.

Figure 6-12

You will see the information screen indicating the features that will be enabled for users who are using Adobe Reader. Besides save form data, users can also use comment and mark-up tools, sign an existing signature field and digitally sign the document (with Adobe Reader 8.0). Once you click on "**Save Now,**" these functionalities will be available.

Figure 6-13

Setting Form Preferences

After you open your interactive PDF form inside Adobe Acrobat 8 Professional, you can set form preferences from **Edit → Preferences...** or by using the shortcut keys [**Ctrl + K**] in Windows Operating Systems. In Mac Operating Systems, you can set form preferences from the **Acrobat → Preferences...**

menu option. Form preferences are divided into three sections: General, Highlight Color and Auto Complete. There are three states of the Auto Complete section: Off, Basic and Advanced. By default, Auto Complete is set to Basic.

Figure 6-14

Using PDF Forms

When you are using interactive PDF forms, you should see your cursor change into a finger pointer or a hand-plus-pointer when you place your mouse pointer over interactive fields such as a check box, button, or radio button or an item inside the dropdown list. For non-interactive forms, you can type your information by going to the **Tools → Typewriter → Typewriter** to enable the typewriter tool to print your form once you are completed.

Figure 6-15

Check Spelling

You can perform a spell-check on your text when you are

entering your data on the forms. Please note that you will not be able to perform a spell-check on the underlying PDF-form text. With your text selected, right-click in Windows or Control-click in Mac OS to trigger the pop-up menu. Select the **Check spelling...** option.

Figure 6-16

You should see the Check Spelling window with word suggestions for words that are not found in the program dictionary. You can either ignore the suggestions or accept one of them if it is correct.

Figure 6-17

If you like to add new words to your custom dictionary, you can go to **Edit → Check Spelling → Edit Dictionary...** and open up the dictionary editor.

Figure 6-18

Clearing Form Data

If you would like to clear all the form data you have entered, you can use **File → Revert**.

Importing Form Data

You can also import form data from external files by going to **Forms → Manage Form Data → Import Data**. You can then select your data file from the open file dialog box. Files formats that acceptable for import are listed in the Table 6-1.

Table 6-1

File Format	File Extension
Acrobat Form Data Format	FDF
Plain Text	TXT
XML Data Package File	XDP
FormFlow99 Data Files	XDF
Acrobat XFDF	XFDF
Extensible Markup Language	XML

Exporting Form Data

One of the obvious reasons for exporting form data is file size. When you archive forms and data together, the file size is much larger than with form-data alone. The file-size difference is compounded when many people have filled out the same form. For example, a college admissions office may receive three hundred applications on the same form every month. For archive purposes, it makes sense to export that data. When administrators want to see a particular person's form with data, all they have to do is open the blank form and then import the data file.

To export form data, you can go to **Forms → Manage Form Data → Export Data** to start the export process.

Figure 6-19

 Depending on how your PDF form was created, you can export your form-data file in the formats listed in either Table 6-2 or Table 6-3.

Table 6-2

File Format	*File Extension*
XML Data Package File	XDP
Extensible Markup Language	XML

Table 6-3

File Format	*File Extension*
Acrobat Form Data Format	FDF
Plain Text	TXT
Acrobat XFDF	XFDF
Extensible Markup Language	XML

Submitting PDF Forms via E-mail

When you are ready to send your PDF-form data via e-mail, click on the submit button. If you have a default e-mail application, such as Outlook or Lotus Notes, installed and configured, you should see your PDF-form data attached in XML format with the recipient and subject fields filled in. Simply click on the **Send** button to submit your form data.

Figure 6-20

If you want to submit your form data at a later time, you can go to **Forms → <u>Distribute Form...</u>** to open a Form Distribution Options window. Within this window, you can select either the Save or Send Later option.

Figure 6-21

Once you click on OK, you should see the Distribution Form. You can enter the e-mail address to which you want your form data returned. In addition, you can obtain a digital ID from Adobe Partner during this step if you want to ensure that the form is returned securely.

Figure 6-22

Then you can specify the location of your data-collection file.

Figure 6-23

Finally, you can specify the save location for your form.

Figure 6-24

Once you have clicked on the **Done** button, Adobe Acrobat will save your files to their appropriate locations and you should see a confirmation message.

Figure 6-25

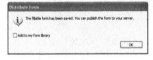

Editing Forms

To edit your PDF form, you can either go to **Forms → Edit Form in Designer...** or use the Edit Layout button on the forms toolbar. If your forms toolbar is not visible and you would like

to make it visible in your workspace, you can go to **Tools →
Customize Toolbars...** to enable it.

Figure 6-26

If you are not the form creator, you can save a copy of your
form and edit on the form copy. Once your form is opened
in editable mode, you can make various changes in Adobe
LiveCycle Designer.

Updating Field Caption or Resizing a Field

If you want to update a field caption, select the field caption,
place your cursor inside the text area, and then update its text.

Figure 6-27

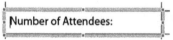

To resize a field, select the field and resize it from the handles
on its border. If the field you want to resize is part of a group of
fields, you will have to ungroup the fields first, and then change
the individual field size.

Adding a E-mail Submit Button

To add a new e-mail submit button, select the E-Mail Submit
button from the standard library and then drag-and-drop it to
the desired location inside your form. You should see a warning
label on the upper right-hand corner of the button indicating
that an e-mail address property has not been set for this button.
To set the e-mail property, select the button (as shown in Figure
6-28), then right-click to trigger the pop-up menu. Select on
Palettes → Object to open the window.

Figure 6-28

When the Object window is opened, you can configure your submit-button properties including e-mail address, subject line, caption, appearance, and other properties. You can even create a rollover caption that is different from its default caption or a different down caption.

Figure 6-29

Adding and Deleting a Field or Object

If you want to add a new field or object to your form, drag-and drop your selected field or object from the library palette to the desired location on your form.

When you want to delete a field or object from your PDF form, select the field or object, then press the Delete key or use the Delete option from the pop-up menu when you right-click on it. You can delete an individual field or object as well as a group of fields or objects.

Summary

In this chapter, we covered three major topics for interactive PDF forms: creating new form, using PDF forms, and editing forms.

You can create new PDF forms from various sources, including scanned paper forms, electronic forms in other formats, or forms created with Adobe LiveCycle Designer. Using Adobe LiveCycle Designer to create a new form was our focus in this chapter.

When using PDF forms, you can check spelling, clear form data, import form data, or export form data. And with the import and export functions, you can save the form data separately from the form layout and archive it. In addition, you can submit your form via e-mail.

You can also edit existing PDF forms. In this section, we discussed updating field captions, resizing a field, adding an e-mail submit button, and adding or deleting a field or object.

7

Document Security

We all have to safeguard our documents for various reasons: protecting customers' privacy in accordance with the law, preventing documents from being accessed by the wrong people, reducing security risks, and much more. Adobe Acrobat 8 Professional has many document security features to satisfy your organization's security requirements.

First, we will cover how to protect your document with a password. You can prevent unauthorized users from opening your document with a password protection. You can further protect your document with a password protection for editing and printing.

Second, we will discuss how to create and use a digital ID. A digital ID is similar to other physical forms of identification you have such as a passport or a birth certificate. Your digital ID has your personalized information, and it authenticates your identity.

Finally, we will focus on digital signatures. You can sign your document digitally with your signature just like you can sign a printed document with your pen. A digital signature is encrypted with a digital ID, and its validity status is shown to users. In this section, you can create your own digital signature image and sign your document.

Once you have experienced how easy it is to secure your PDF document, you will be able to apply these skills to protect your sensitive data.

Password Protection

Using a password to protect your document is a frequently used security feature in many applications, including Adobe Acrobat 8 Professional. There are two password protection options in Adobe Acrobat 8 Professional: a password for opening the document and a password for printing and editing the document. To protect your document with a password, you can use the secure menu and then select the **Password Encrypt...** option.

Figure 7-1

When you use this feature for the first time, you should see an "Apply New Security Settings" message.

Figure 7-2

Please note that your compatibility setting affects the encryption level. With compatibility set to Adobe 3 and later, you can have a low encryption level with 40-bit RC4. You can set a high encryption level with 128-bit RC4 or AES by selecting other compatibility options.

On the settings screen, you should be able to check "Require a password to open the document" and "Restrict editing and printing of the document." A password will be required in order to change these permission settings. You can type your password into the password field(s).

Figure 7-3

When the user performs a search, the search engine accesses Metadata to search for results. If you select the "Encrypt all document contents" option, the document contents and Metadata will all be encrypted. With this option, the user will not be able to perform a search because the search engine can not access Metadata. You can select "Encrypt all document contents except Metadata," and the user can perform a search with this option.

Inside the "Printing Allowed" drop-down list, you can select none, low resolution, or high resolution. You can also specify what level of changes users can perform:

- None
- Inserting, deleting, and rotating pages

- Filling in form fields and signing existing signature fields
- Commenting, filling in form fields, and signing existing signature fields
- Any, except extracting pages

Once you click on the **OK** button, you will be asked to confirm the password.

Figure 7-4

You will also be alerted with a warning messaging indicating that the password protection can be bypassed by third-party products. You can disable this message window.

Figure 7-5

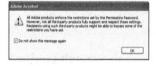

Once your document is password protected, you should see the security lock icon on the security permissions property link and on the document creator.

Figure 7-6

When you click on the Permission Details hyperlink, you will open the document's security properties window. You can view the document restrictions summary here.

Figure 7-7

To ensure your security setting changes take effect, you have to save your document prior to exiting the document. The next time any user tries to open the document, he/she will be asked to provide a password.

Figure 7-8

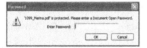

Encrypting Document with Digital ID

When you encrypt your document with digital ID, you can specify different permissions for different groups. For example, you can allow a customer service representative to view a claim form and allow his or her manager to edit and sign it. A digital ID contains two keys: a public key and a private key. The public key is known to everyone, and the private key is known only to an individual user. You can use the public key to verify a digital signature or encrypt a document, and you can use the private key to create a digital signature or decrypt a document.

Your digital ID is similar to your real-life identification, such as driver license, as it contains your personal information and expiration date. In essence, you use the public key to lock data and the private key to unlock data.

To encrypt a PDF document, you need to have a digital ID generated either by a third party or yourself. Self-generated digital ID can be problematic: If you lose your digital ID, the document is no longer accessible. Therefore, you should be very careful with your digital ID storage. With a digital ID generated by a third-party provider—certificate authority (CA)—you can request a replacement digital ID to open the document. Many business-to-business transactions or document-sharing activities require a digital ID from a trusted CA.

To manage your digital IDs in Adobe Acrobat 8 Professional, you can go to **Advanced → Security Settings** to open the Security Settings window. In this window, you can add, review, remove, share, and export digital IDs. You can also configure directory servers, time-stamp servers, and Adobe LiveCycle Servers.

Figure 7-9

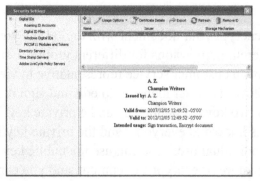

If you need a new digital ID, you can click on the plus sign to add a digital ID. There are four options for creating a digital ID: browse for an existing digital ID file, configure a roaming ID for use on this computer, create a self-signed digital ID for use with Acrobat, and look for newly inserted hardware tokens.

Figure 7-10

The standard file format for digital ID is PKCS #12. In Windows, the file extension is .pfx and in Mac OS the file extension is .p12. You can also choose Windows certificate store to integrate with your Windows login credentials.

Figure 7-11

Then, you can provide your personal identification information.

Figure 7-12

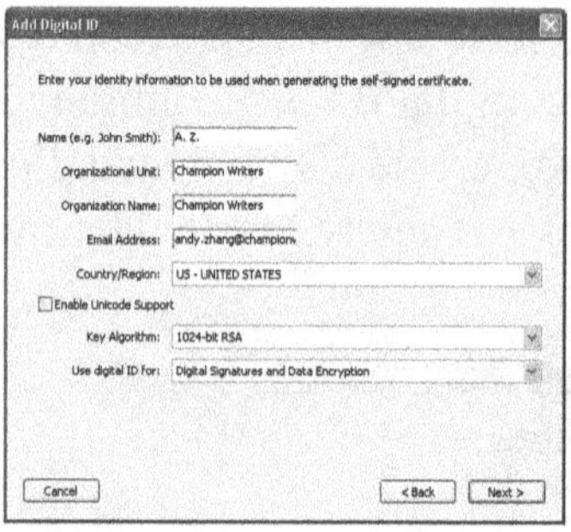

Finally, you can supply a password for this digital ID. Whenever you want to delete this digital ID, you will have to provide the same password.

Figure 7-13

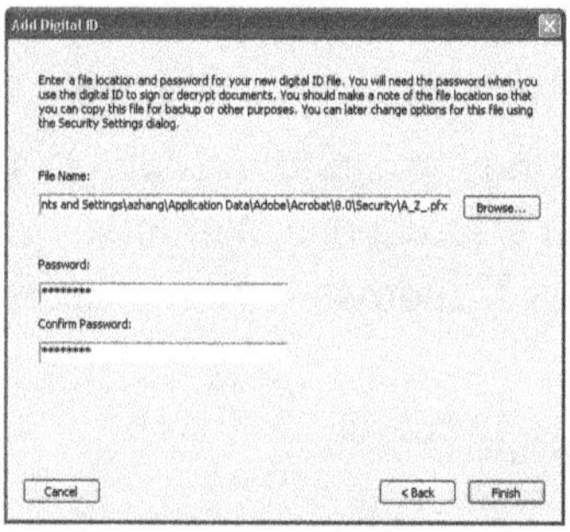

When you have at least one digital ID, you can encrypt your document with your selected digital ID. You can go to **Secure → 1 Certificate Encrypt...** to start the process.

Figure 7-14

There are three steps in the certificate security settings process: general settings, select recipients, and summary. During the general settings step, you can specify certificate security policy, select components to encrypt, and choose an encryption algorithm.

Figure 7-15

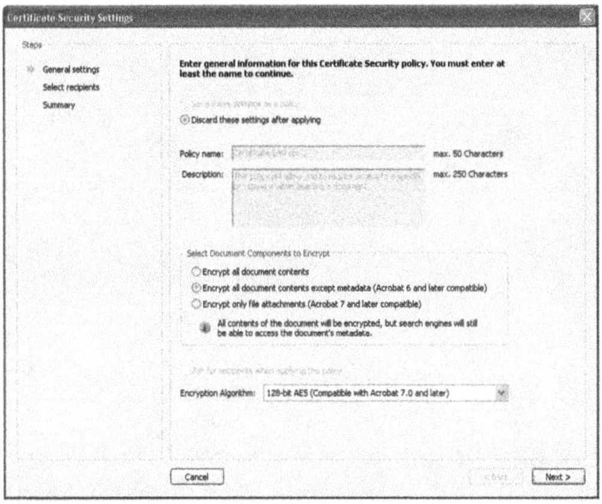

During the step of selecting recipients, you can search, browse, add, and remove recipients from your directory. You can also set document restrictions by clicking on the **Permissions...** button.

Figure 7-16

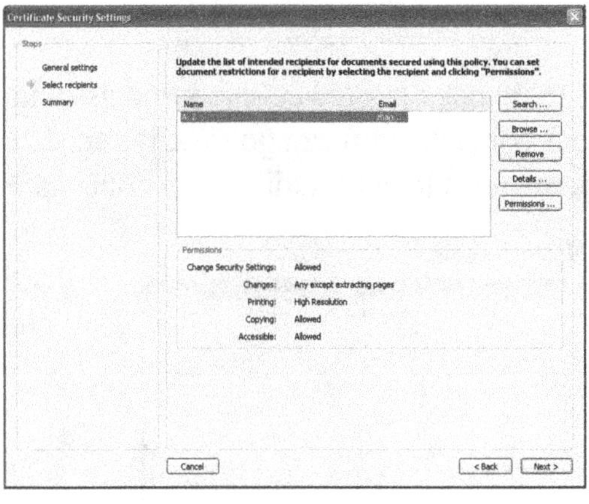

Finally, you can review your summary information and complete your process. After you click on the **Finish** button and save your document, your document will be encrypted.

Figure 7-17

Once your document has been encrypted with digital ID, you can open the document only with the proper digital ID and password.

Figure 7-18

If you want to manage trusted contacts and associate digital IDs with your contacts, you can go to **Advanced → Manage Trusted Identities...** to start adding new contacts or groups.

Figure 7-19

Digital Signatures

A digital signature resembles a real signature in many ways; you sign a document with your digital signature to authenticate a document or approve it. A digital signature is encrypted with digital ID, and its validity status is shown to users. You can use either a signature image or your user name to digitally sign your documents. In this section, we will cover how to create a digital signature and how to digitally sign a document.

Create a Digital Signature

Before you sign a digital signature, you should have a digital ID. Your signature image can be your scanned handwritten signature, another image you choose, or simply your name. Once your image is ready, you can go to **Edit → Preferences** in Windows or **Acrobat → Preferences** in Mac OS. Once the preferences window is opened, you can navigate to **Security** section. To attach your image as your signature image, you can click on **New...** button.

Figure 7-20

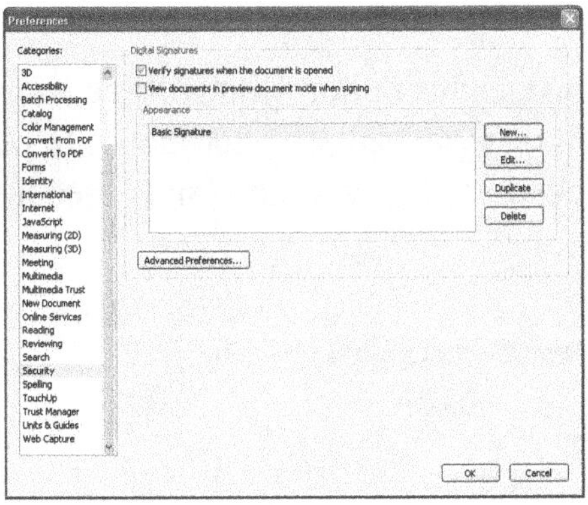

If you select **Imported Graphic**, you can click on **File...** to attach your signature image.

Figure 7-21

After you completed this process, you can place you signature in your PDF document. To start signing your document, you can click on **Sign** button on the task bar and choose **Place Signature...** option.

Figure 7-22

The first time you use this option, you will see an information box showing you that you can use your mouse to place your signature by click, drag, or draw the desired area inside your document.

Figure 7-23

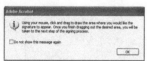

To digitally sign your document, you will need a digital ID. If you already have a digital ID and you would like to use that ID, then you can just browse to the digital ID file. Otherwise, you can configure a roaming ID or create a self-signed digital ID. Another option is to look for newly inserted hardware tokens.

Figure 7-24

Once you have your digital ID ready, you can provide your password and click on **Next** to continue.

Figure 7-25

You should see your digital ID has been added to the list and it is ready to be used for signing your document.

Figure 7-26

The Sign Document window will come up with your available digital signatures, you can click on **Sign** to place your digital signature into your PDF document.

Figure 7-27

You will be asked to save your changes for your document. Once you have saved your document, you should see your digital signature has been placed in your document.

Figure 7-28

When users click on the digital signature, they should see a signature validation status showing the authenticity of the signature. The pen with a check mark sign indicates the digital signature is valid. If the signature is invalid, you should see red X icon; if the document has been changed after it has been digitally signed, then you should see a caution triangle icon. When Adobe Acrobat cannot validate a digital signature, you should see a question mark.

Figure 7-29

When a user opens the digitally signed document, he/she can also see the digital signature from the Signature panel. You can click on **Options** menu to access all the available menu options. For example, if your current version of the document is different from the signed version, you can compare these two versions by clicking on **Compare Signed Version to Current Version**.

Figure 7-30

Advanced Preferences for Digital Signature

If you would like to further customize your digital signature, you can go to **Edit → Preferences** in Windows or **Acrobat → Preferences** in Mac OS. Once the preferences window is opened, you can navigate to **Security** section and click on **Advanced Preferences** button. There are three tabs available: verification, creation, and Windows integration.

In the verification tab, you can specify what verification method should be used and the frequency of verification.

Figure 7-31

At the creation tab, you can select the default method for signing and encrypting your document, whether to include revocation status, and other options.

Figure 7-32

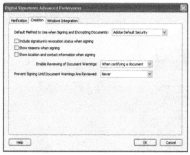

 If you would like to integrate with Windows certificate store to include Windows certificates, you can enable this capability at the Windows integration tab.

Figure 7-33

Summary

Protecting your sensitive information is an important task for document creators and users. In this chapter, we explored the security features inside Adobe Acrobat 8 Professional including password protection, encrypting documents with digital ID, and signing your documents with digital signatures. Some applications offer password protection to open the document but not password protection to edit or print the document. Adobe Acrobat 8 Professional offers both types of password protection.

You can also encrypt your PDF document with a digital ID. Inside Adobe Acrobat 8 Professional, you can create a new digital ID or use an existing digital ID. You can also sign a document manually with a digital signature just like using a pen. A digital signature is also encrypted with digital ID and its validity is available to users. With all these security features, you can create, view, and share documents with confidence.

8

Creating Accessible Documents

It is estimated that over forty million users worldwide are either blind or visually impaired. Therefore, creating PDF documents with greater accessibility should be not just a goal to satisfy government regulations or requirements; it is essential to satisfy your users. When we covered creating PDF forms in Chapter 6, we discussed how to create a tool-tip text property that tags to form fields such as a text box or drop-down list. In this chapter, we will discuss how to improve accessibility in your PDF documents.

To know your document's accessibility, you can perform an accessibility check. There are two types of accessibility checks: quick check and full check. Once you have completed your accessibility check, you can review accessibility issues in the accessibility report. You can consider improving your document's accessibility based on the report findings.

In this chapter, we are going to cover some important aspects of accessibility, including adding tags, setting document language, arranging reading order, adding alternate text for images, shapes, and form fields, and adjusting your security settings to allow accessibility. At the end of this chapter, we will introduce Adobe Acrobat 8 Professional's Read Out Loud feature.

Validate Accessibility

Performing the Accessibility Check

To ensure that your document is accessible to visually impaired or motion challenged users, you can perform an accessibility check. There are two types of accessibility check: quick check and full check. A full accessibility check may take a few minutes—depending on the length or complexity of your document. If you want to get an idea about your document's accessibility, you can choose quick check. To start a full accessibility check, you can go to **Advanced → Accessibility → Full Check**.

Quick Check will examine your PDF document and check its searchable text, and document structure tags and security settings to allow screen reader applications to access. To start a quick accessibility check, you can go to **Advanced → Accessibility → Quick Check**. In Windows, you can use shortcut keys [**Shift + Ctrl + 6**]. If you use Mac OS, you can use [**Shift + Command + 6**].

Figure 8-1

Once your check process is completed, you should be able to see an information summary window generated by the accessibility checker.

Figure 8-2

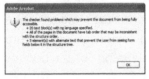

You should find your Accessibility Report in the navigation pane. The report includes a detailed report with errors found in the document, a summary, repair hints, and a legal disclaimer.

Figure 8-2

Checking Tagged PDF Property

When a user cannot see or interpret visual elements, he/she can depend on an assistive software package to provide information based on document structure tags. If a document is well structured with meaningful tags, the assistive software can produce alternative output such as sound to help the user to understand and interpret the meanings of the document. When tags are absent from a document, assistive software will either be unable to provide information in the correct order or able to provide nothing at all. Another benefit of well-structured tags in a PDF document is content rearrangement. When the user views the document from a small portable device such as a pocket PC, the mobile device will rearrange the document according to the document tags. Without proper document tags, the document will likely not be displayed correctly.

The good news is that Adobe Acrobat 8 Professional will automatically add document tags by default when you are creating your document. To verify if your document is set to

Yes for Tagged PDF document property, you can go to **File** → **Properties** or [**Ctrl** + **D**] to open the Document Properties window. In the Description tab, you should see an Advanced pane at the bottom of the window. You can validate the Tagged PDF property setting here.

Figure 8-3

You should keep accessibility in mind when you are creating PDF documents. Actually, it is better to integrate accessibility as one of the key considerations in your planning stage. You can consider some typical accessibility issues, including creating alternative text for graphical elements, ensuring document structure can be converted into tags by using document structure features such as paragraph styles, and preparing to optimize tables.

When your document contains form fields, you should ensure that these fields are interactive and have descriptions associated with them. To validate the status of these fields in your document, you can perform an analysis by going to **Forms** → **Run Form** → **Field Recognition** in Adobe Acrobat 8 Professional. You should see a recognition report with detected form fields and their status. Based on the report, you can perform repairs to these undefined fields.

Figure 8-4

Adding Tags

There are two ways of adding tags to your PDF document: 1) from the authoring application or 2) after the PDF document has been created. If you create your document from Adobe Acrobat 8 Professional, your document should contain tags by default. If you have a PDF document without tags, you can add tags to your document as an additional step. (Please note that if the document has some existing tags, this process will clear them out prior to adding new tags.) To add tags to your document, you can go to **Advanced → Accessibility Add Tags to Document**. During this process, Adobe Acrobat will analyze the document structure, including text alignment, tables, columns, links, and bookmarks, then covert them into proper tag hierarchy. If there are issues while adding tags to your document, an error report will appear in the navigation pane under Adding Tags Report.

Figure 8-5

Setting Document Language

If a document has its document language properly setup, then screen reader applications can easily switch to the designated language. With Adobe Acrobat 8 Professional, you can set document language for the entire document or for a portion of the document.

Setting Document Language for the Entire Document

To set document language for the entire document, you can go to **File → Properties** or use the shortcut key [**Ctrl** + **D**], then navigate the Advanced tab. Inside the Reading Options pane, you should see the languages dropdown list where you can select the appropriate language for the document.

Figure 8-6

If you can not find the language you want from the dropdown list, you can enter the ISO 639 code instead. You can search for ISO 639 language code from the Library of Congress web site for ISO 639 standard web site at:

http://www.loc.gov/standards/iso639-2/langhome.html

Figure 8-7

Setting Document Language for Portions of the Document

To set document language for a section of document text, you can use the TouchUp Text tool from the Advance Editing toolbar, which is a convenient way of editing your tags for a section of text. You will need to select the text, then right click to open the properties window.

Figure 8-8

You can navigate the Tags tab, then choose your desired language here.

Figure 8-9

Arranging Reading Order

Reading order determines the sequence of document elements that will be available to users. If your reading order is different from your layout order, then visually impaired users will be confused when they rely on other applications to read your document. Therefore, it is essential to make sure your reading order is correct. To check your reading order, you can use the TouchUp Reading Order tool, which can be found in the Advance Editing toolbar next to the TouchUp Text tool. To check your reading order, you must first select the TouchUp Reading Order tool, and then select the document elements that you want to review. The TouchUp Reading Order screen should appear, and you should click on the Show Order Panel button to see reading orders within the document.

Figure 8-10

You can easily make appropriate changes to your reading orders with the Order tab. You can also make other changes here such as Tags, Contents, and Fields.

Figure 8-11

Adding Alternate Text

Alternate text for shapes and images is a highly effective navigational aid for nongraphical and audio users because they are dependent on the alternate text to provide information. You can use the TouchUp Object tool from the Advance Editing toolbar to add and edit alternate text to shapes and images.

Figure 8-12

Allowing Screen Reader Applications to Access Document

Screen reader applications must extract or copy data from your document then convert it into speech. However, your security settings can interfere with screen reader applications when you deny the user the ability to copy or extract data from your document. If you are setting low-encryption-level security for your document, you can choose the following option when you set password security: Enable Copying of Text, Images, and Other Content. If you are setting low-encryption-level security for your document, you can choose the following option when you set password security: Enable Text Access for Screen Reader Devices for the Visually Impaired. These settings allow screen reader applications to access document content.

Figure 8-13

Read Out Loud

A great way to review your document's tags and reading orders is to activate Read Out Loud. The Read Out Loud feature reads your PDF document, and covers content text, comments, and alternate text for shapes, images, and form fields in reading orders. It will also give you an overview of your document accessibility. You can go to **View → Read Out Loud** or use shortcut keys [**Shift** + **Ctrl** + **Y**] to activate or deactivate the feature.

Figure 8-14

Summary

In this chapter, we covered some accessibility topics related to creating a PDF document. Visually impaired or motion challenged users are usually dependant on screen reader applications to access your document. Therefore, it is critical for you to create your PDF document with accessibility as a priority, especially if you are going to share your document with numerous users. We started this chapter with accessibility checks, which you can perform as a quick or a full check.

If your document spans over multiple pages, tagging can help users follow the content flow sequentially. We covered how to add tags to your document, and discussed how to set document language for the entire document or for a portion of the document. We introduced reading order and alternate text, and we covered how your document security setting can affect accessibility. Finally, this chapter included information for the Read Out Loud feature. All of these features are essential settings that allow the user to access your document.

9

Adding Audio, Video, and 3D Models

Adobe Acrobat 8 Professional is a rich multimedia environment that can incorporate audio, video, and 3D models into a PDF document. Files can be added and played by any compatible media player. Adobe Acrobat 8 Professional currently supports these media players: Adobe Flash Player, QuickTime, RealPlayer, and Windows Media Player.

We start this chapter with an introduction on how to add audio or video objects into a PDF document. These tools are available from Advanced Editing Toolbox, and these objects can be positioned at your discretion. You can also make an object invisible if you choose.

Later, we discuss how to add new renditions. Each media player application supports some video formats, but none supports all of them. Also, users have different system settings and configurations, which makes additional renditions ideal in order to offer users an optimized viewing experience.

Finally, we cover how to add 3D model files into a PDF document by using the 3D object tool. In addition, we include some resources for further reading in case you work extensively with 3D models and Adobe Acrobat.

Adding Audio or Video

To add an audio or video file to a PDF document, click on either the Sound or Movie Tool from alternate text Toolbox, then place the cursor at the desired position. If you don't see Advanced Editing Toolbox, go to **Tools → Customize Toolbars...** to enable it.

Figure 9-1

Next, choose Acrobat 6 (and later) or Acrobat 5 (and later) compatible media for your multimedia content. Acrobat 6 (and later) compatible media support more file formats and options, including Embed the Movie and Create Multiple Renditions. If you choose the Acrobat 6 (and later) compatible media option to play a multimedia file, you must have Acrobat 6 (and later), or download and install the current version of Adobe Acrobat Reader.

Figure 9-2

Once you click on **OK**, a rectangle box is placed on the position you previously selected. When you double-click on the object rectangle, you open the Multimedia Properties window. The Settings tab gives the options for Annotation Title, Alternate Text, and Rendition Settings. Always add alternate text for your multimedia file for accessibility.

Figure 9-3

 The Appearance tab gives you the options to customize the object place holder appearance. You can also make your object invisible if you choose.

Figure 9-4

The Actions tab gives you the options to configure Trigger (such as Mouse Up or Page Visible) and Action (such as Play a Sound or Play Media).

Figure 9-5

When you mouse over your multimedia file object, you will notice the cursor has changed into a hand symbol. Once you click on it, you should see a security alert window asking you about the play option: Play this multimedia content this one time, or play this multimedia content and add this document to my list of trusted documents.

Figure 9-6

Once you click on **Play**, this multimedia file will start to play with your available media player.

Creating Multiple Renditions

You can save a video into many different formats. The term "rendition" means output format. Because users have different media players and each media player supports a limited number of formats, sometimes it is necessary to create multiple renditions for a video. Rendition is assigned for Mouse Up event by default. Rendition is played as soon as the mouse is clicked and released with Mouse Up event. You can change to a different event if desired.

Figure 9-7

When you are ready to add new renditions, click on Add Rendition. You can add new renditions either from a file or from a URL.

Figure 9-8

Once your new rendition file and specified system properties are added, you should see the new rendition listed inside the renditions list. You can move the play order up and down for these renditions, if needed. When you want to watch the video, the rendition will be played according to user's system configuration and properties.

Figure 9-9

Adding 3D Models

This section will cover how to add 3D models into a PDF document. From the Advanced Editing Toolbar, you can select 3D Object Tool and click on your desired position inside the document to add your 3D model.

Figure 9-10

The Add 3D Content window allows you to select the 3D model file, configure navigation and display properties, and choose a poster option. Within the Navigation and Display pane, you can set default background color, lighting, rendering style, animation style, default views, or an open model tree by default.

Figure 9-11

Once your 3D model has been successfully added into your PDF document, right-click on the model and choose Properties to open the 3D Properties window. You can configure interface settings and activation settings here.

Figure 9-12

There is so much information about 3D model and this topic itself can make into a book itself. If you like to read more about 3D object and Adobe Acrobat, you can review the following PDF document from Adobe web site—*Get started with intelligent 3D Adobe PDF documents*. The current URL is:

http://www.adobe.com/designcenter/acrobat3d/articles/ac3dit_workflow08/ac3dit_workflow08.pdf

Another document you can review is *Create interactive 3D documentation*. The current URL is:

http://www.adobe.com/designcenter/acrobat3d/articles/ac3dit_3dtechpub/ac3dit_3dtechpub.pdf

Finally, for users want to create PDF documents from CAD applications, the following document is useful: *Capture a 3D PDF file from your CAD application*. The URL is:

http://www.adobe.com/designcenter/acrobat3d/articles/ac3dit_capture/ac3dit_capture.pdf

Summary

In this chapter, we covered the following topics: adding audio and video, creating multiple renditions, and adding 3D models into a PDF document. With tools from Advanced Editing Toolbar, you can easily add music, movies, and 3D animation models into your document. These multimedia objects will enhance your document and provide a rich user experience. Because users have different system configurations, you can also add different renditions to your video settings, allowing users to watch your video with the best possible view.

This chapter merely touches on the basics of 3D models with a PDF document. At the end of this chapter, we include some documents from Adobe with more information about Acrobat 3D, as well as other useful information about 3D models, CAD applications, and others.

10

Perform Searching and Indexing

We will cover searching and indexing in this chapter. Adobe Acrobat 8 Professional provides basic search features, such as whole-word search, case sensitivity selection, and bookmarks and comments searching. The Advanced Search window allows you to see your search keywords within the document context. You can toggle between Basic Search and Advanced Search with a click on the link.

We will also introduce some search functions, such as stemming, proximity, and Boolean query. If you would like to perform a search based on a part of a word, then you can consider using the stemming option. When you want to perform a search on two keywords separated by a range of words, then you can use the proximity feature. You can also use a search query to perform a custom search. We will cover some commonly used Boolean query operators.

Indexing can decrease the time needed to search a document. In the indexing section, we will introduce how to perform indexing on a document. You can also update an index file or build an index file based on a collection of files—a catalog. A catalog can be composed of files from different directories. When you create a catalog, all files in the catalog share the same index file. If you perform a search on this catalog, you can really speed up the search process. In this section, we will also cover how to rebuild the index and update a catalog. And last, we will discuss how to incorporate document metadata into your search and index task.

Searching

To perform a text search, type your search phrase into the Find text box, and you should see a list of options: Whole words only, Case-Sensitive, Include Bookmarks, and Include Comments. If you select Whole words only, the search engine only looks for the entire search phrase, not individual words. The Case-Sensitive option lets you find the search phrase with exact capitalization.

 If you select Include Bookmarks, the search engine will search the document content along with text inside the bookmark pane. The same principle applies to the Include Comments option; once it is selected, the search engine will search content text along with comment text. When you click on these options, you should see a checkmark in front of the options you have selected.

Figure 10-1

When you want to open the full Acrobat search window, you can click on **Open Full Acrobat Search...** or use shortcut keys **[Shift + Ctrl + F]**. This window has more options to perform a search, including searching documents in a different directory.

Figure 10-2

As soon as you start your search, you can find Search Previous and Search Next buttons next to the Find text box. These buttons are very convenient for navigation.

Figure 10-3

One of my favorite features in Adobe Acrobat is the results list in the full search window. You can scroll up and down the list to see your searched text within context, then click on the specific instance of your search list and jump to that section of the content.

Figure 10-4

The Advanced Search options also allow you to either search exact phrases or any word inside the search phrase. Furthermore, you can select search attachments in addition to the content text. You can toggle between Advanced Search and Basic Search from the hyperlink at the bottom of the search form.

Figure 10-5

Stemming

You can create a stem—part of a word. For example, *inter* can be a stem for words like *international* and *interstate*. To search words containing your search stem, you can check the Stemming option inside Advanced Search. Obviously, you can't use Stemming in conjunction with Whole words and Case-Sensitive searching.

Proximity

If you are looking for two key words that are separated by no more than a specific number of words in between, then you can use the Proximity option. You can perform a Proximity search only when you are using Match All of the words search option. The Proximity search can be performed for multiple documents or index definition files but is not available for single PDF document.

Figure 10-6

You can also add additional criteria into your search from the additional criteria dropdown list, combined with the choices Contains or Does not contain and the text box. These criteria include Date Created, Date Modified, Author, Title, Subject, Filename, Keywords, Bookmarks, Comments, JPEG Images, XMP Metadata, and Object Data.

Figure 10-7

Boolean Query

You can add a customized Boolean query into your search phrase. If you have used query language in other environments such as a database, constructing a Boolean query should be easy for you. You can find more information about queries from many resources in this topic. There are several query operators you can use, and here are some examples:

OR

If you are trying to find occurrences of either term, you can use the OR operator. For example, you can your document for "reeducation or re-education" and the OR operator will return results with either term.

Exclusive OR: ^

When you want to search for occurrences of any one term but not both terms together, you can use the exclusive or operator ^ to separate two terms. For example, you can search "Hawaii ^ Guam" to find documents containing either Hawaii or Guam. If a document has both Hawaii and Guam, then it will not be returned.

NOT

If you don't want to find a particular term in your search, you can include the NOT operator. For example, you can use "NOT component" to exclude any document that contains the term "component."

( )

When you are building a complex query, you can use parentheses to set the evaluation order for the search engine. Terms inside parentheses will be evaluated first. For example, you can use the search term "Business AND (Component OR Object)" to get results for Component and Business or Object and Business. The query inside the parentheses is evaluated first, then it combines with the rest of the query.

Figure 10-8

Indexing

When implemented properly, it usually takes less time to search for an indexed document than a non-indexed document. Indexing can be especially effective for lengthy documents. Once documents are indexed, Adobe Acrobat can perform a speedy search with the embedded index. For shared or distributed PDF documents, the embedded index is available to all users. Users can perform searches in documents with embedded indices the same way they would with non-index documents.

Performing an Index

To perform an index on your document, you can go to **A**dvanced → **D**ocument Processing → **Manage Embedded Index** to start the process. If your document does not have an embedded index, find the **Embed Index** button. Click on the button to start the indexing process.

Figure 10-9

Once your indexing process is completed, you should be able to either remove or update your index.

Figure 10-10

Updating Index and Building Catalogs

When you need to update your index, you can go to **Advanced → Document Processing → Full Text Index with Catalog** to open the update window. To update an existing index, click on the **Open Index** button. From the open file dialog window you can select your catalog index file with a .pdx extension.

Figure 10-11

With your index file opened, you can make any necessary changes such as building, rebuilding, or purging the file. You can also include or exclude directories. You can build an index for a collection of files from different directories by building a catalog. A catalog is a group of files that share a standard index. When the user searches a catalog instead of each individual file, the search process is optimized.

Figure 10-12

Setting Catalog Preferences

In Windows, you can go to **Edit → Preferences** or **[Ctrl + K]** to open the preferences window, then select **Catalog** inside the Categories list. If you are using Mac OS, you can go to **Acrobat → Preferences**.

Figure 10-13

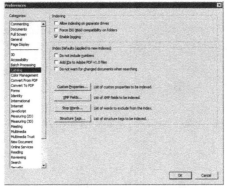

Document Metadata

Your document metadata is another aspect of indexing and searching. Metadata makes your PDF file easy to search. document metadata has several fields including file, subject, keyword, author, and copyright-related information. To update your document metadata, go to **File → Properties** then open the description tab.

Figure 10-14

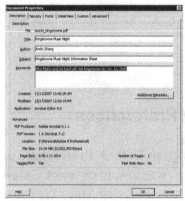

To add copyright information and other advanced settings, click on the **Additional Metadata** button to open the metadata window.

Figure 10-15

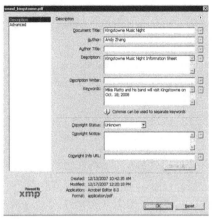

Summary

In this chapter, we covered two topics: searching and indexing. Both features are easy to use. In the searching section, we covered stemming—using a portion of a word to perform a search; proximity—finding words within a range; and constructing search queries. We also introduced other features such as basic and advanced search options.

Indexing can accelerate the search process, and the time saving itself is a good incentive to index your document. In the indexing section, we covered how to perform indexing, how to update an index file, and how to build catalogs. A catalog is a group of files based on the same unified index file. We also discussed how to set catalog preferences. Finally, we covered how to update your document metadata.

The Pocket Book of Adobe Acrobat 8 Professional

11

Printing and Production

In this chapter, we are going to cover a crucial aspect of PDF documents: print and production. After you've spent hours creating your document, you'll want to make sure it looks great in print. Adobe Acrobat 8 Professional provides many tools for the print and production process.

We begin this chapter by introducing how to print your document in Adobe Acrobat. You can configure your page, printer, and paper layout properties from the print menu. We will also discuss how to print a selected area on a page. In addition to printing your document, you can also print bookmarks, comments, and attachments. We will also introduce PostScript Printer Description (PPD) files.

The heart and soul of Adobe Acrobat 8 Professional for print and production are print production tools. These tools are available on the Print Production Toolbar and as an advanced menu item. Print and production tools covered in this chapter include: Trap Presets, Output Preview, Preflight, Convert Colors, Ink Manager, Add Printer Marks, Crop Pages, Fix Hairlines, Transparency Flattening, PDF Optimizer, and PDF Job Definitions. Each print and production tool has numerous settings you can modify to meet your print and production environment requirements.

Print Your Document

Before you print your document, you can go to **File →
Print Setup** (or by using shortcut keys [**Shift** + **Ctrl** + **P**] in
Windows or **File → Page Setup** in Mac OS) to make sure
your page settings are correct. To view more page and printing
properties, you can click on the **Properties** button to open the
Print Properties window.

Figure 11-1

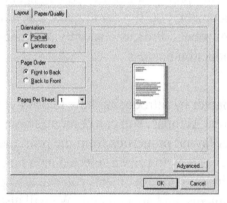

To print your document, you can either click on the **Print**
button on the toolbar, go to **File → Print**, or use shortcut keys
[**Ctrl** + **P**].

Figure 11-2

You should see the Print Properties window open, displaying
typical print properties for your printer.

Figure 11-3

If you need to manage output color, ink, and print marks, you can click on the A**d**vanced button to open the Advanced Print Setup window. When you choose Reverse pages, your printer will print the last page first. Inside the Page Handling pane, you can choose how to scale your page. Your document can be enlarged or shrunk into a printable area or to fit your paper size. For example, if you have an oversized document, you can shrink the document so it will fit into your paper size.

Figure 11-4

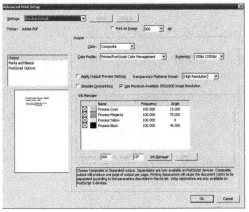

Print Preset

If you have a stable printing environment and you want to save time setting printing properties, you can perform print preset—saving your default print settings. To perform print preset, you can go to **File → Properties** or use shortcut keys [**Ctrl + D**] to open the Properties window. Next, go to the Advanced tab, where you can configure your print preset inside the Print Dialog Presets pane.

Figure 11-5

Print Selected Area on a Page

With Acrobat Professional 8, you can take a snapshot of a portion of your page or your entire page. To take a snapshot, go to **Tools → Select & Zoom**, and then select the **Snapshot Tool**.

Figure 11-6

You should see your mouse pointer turn into a crosshair and you can drag the crosshair over the area where you want a snapshot taken. Your selected snapshot area will be inside the dark rectangle and the colors inside the rectangle will be temporarily inverted. You should see an alert message saying, "the selected area has been copied," if the alert box has not been disabled. You can disable this message so it will not show up in the future.

Figure 11-7

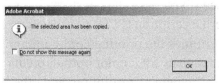

When you are ready to print this portion of your page, you can go to **File → Print** or use shortcut keys [**Ctrl + P**]. When the Print window opens, you should see inside the Print Range pane, the selected graphic option is selected by default. You can also see the preview composite with only the selected portion of your page inside the Preview pane. You can also find the Booklet Printing option from the Page Scaling dropdown list. Your printer must support manual or automatic duplex printing in order to print booklets.

Figure 11-8

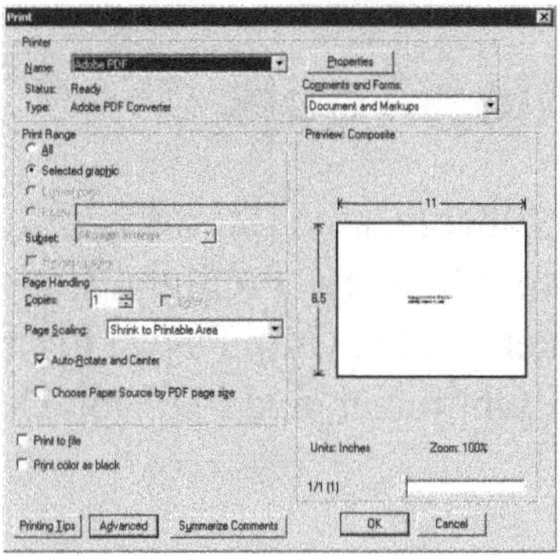

Print Bookmark

You can open the bookmark navigation pane and select one or multiple bookmarks by using [**Ctrl**] and by clicking the bookmarks. With your bookmarks selected, you can go to the Print menu and print your bookmarks.

PostScript Printer Description File

If your printout does not look ideal, you may need to investigate and see if you have the latest version of the PostScript Printer Description (PPD) file for your printer. The PPD file determines the printing configuration for your PostScript printer such as font, color output, media sizes, page orientation, screen frequency, resolution, and other properties. To add a PPD file in Windows, select Add Printer from the Control Panel. In Mac OS, select Add in the Printer List window.

Figure 11-9

Print Production Tools

The Print Production toolbar has the following print production tools: Trap Presets, Output Preview, Preflight, Convert Colors, Ink Manager, Add Printer Marks, Crop Pages, Fix Hairlines, Flattener Preview, PDF Optimizer, and PDF Job Definitions.

Figure 11-10

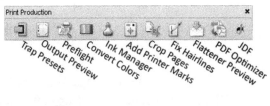

If you don't see the print production toolbar, you can go to
Tools → Customize Toolbars to open the More Tools screen.
Then select the Print Production toolbar.

Figure 11-11

In this section, we will briefly explain the usage for these tools.

Trap Presets

In the ideal world, each ink cartridge is perfectly aligned so
the output has no misregistration of any object. However, each
printing process varies, and you may find undesirable gaps
between different objects with different colors. To compensate
these tiny gaps, you can set the spread of each object to spread
slightly with the adjacent object of a different color. This

process is called *trapping*. Ink trapping is used to prevent misregistration in the printing process by overlapping the colors around the object edge where two objects with different colors meet.

You can save your trap configuration settings with the Trap Presets tool. When you execute these trap settings later, you can use Adobe PostScript 3 RIP which licenses Adobe In-RIP Trapping.

Figure 11-12

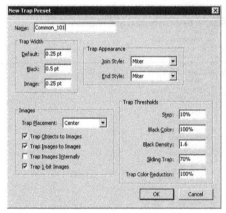

To add new trap settings, you can click on the Create button.

Figure 11-13

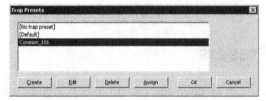

Output Preview

You can preview your production output using numerous simulation profiles available from the dropdown list, simulate

black ink, simulate paper color, select Ink Manager, use Separation Preview, and activate color warnings. The output preview allows you to visualize how your printout will look under different conditions. Some simulation profiles allow you to choose which color to show for your preview.

Figure 11-14

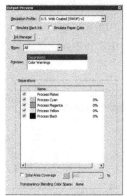

Preflight

During the preflight phase, you can check your content and make sure all elements are correctly configured on your page, find any compatibility or output issues, and fix these issues before production. There are more than 400 predefined tasks for the preflight check. During the preflight check, Adobe Acrobat will check your document against the preflight profile. You can customize your preflight profile to ensure it meets your specific requirements. There are three important tasks you can perform during the preflight phase to ensure production quality:

▪   If you are going to submit your document to a four-color printing facility, you should consider converting your colors into the CMYK or Device N color scheme. You can reference the Convert Colors section to convert your colors.

- Because not all applications support the same set of fonts, you should embed your fonts inside Adobe Acrobat to ensure they will not to be substituted during production.

- When you create your document from various applications, be sure that your document is optimized either by the authoring application or by using the properties from your print service provider. You can reference the PDF Optimizer section for more optimization information in Adobe Acrobat 8 Professional.

Figure 11-15

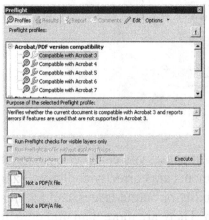

Convert Colors

With your document page range selected, you can convert from Device CMYK, RGB, and Grayscale color spaces into numerous destination color spaces. You also have te option to embed profile.

Figure 11-16

Ink Manager

If you would like to configure the way inks are treated for your document and printout, you can use Ink Manager to manage ink type, neutral density, and trapping sequence. Ink Manager is very useful for print shop because production technician can change spot color into CMYK process color or map two similar colors into one.

Figure 11-17

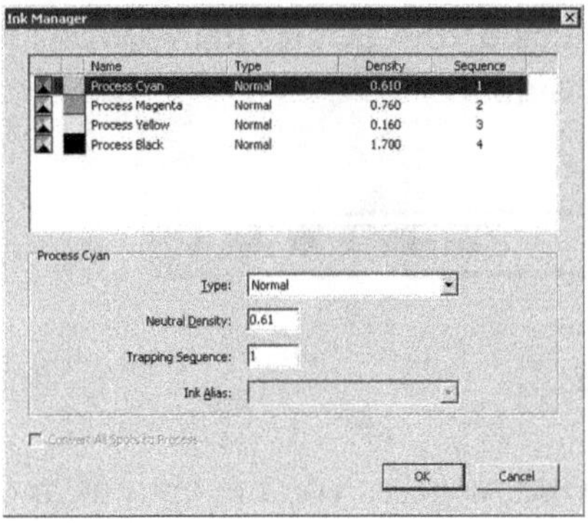

Add Printer Marks

Printer marks—trim, bleed, registration, color bars, page information—are embedded in your PDF documents. When you want to add these printer marks to your output, you can select them from the Add Printer Marks window.

Figure 11-18

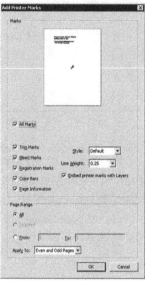

Once you have selected your printer marks, you should see them in your final output.

Figure 11-19

Crop Pages

The Crop Pages window gives you the options to control your crop margins and page size for a selected page range.

Figure 11-20

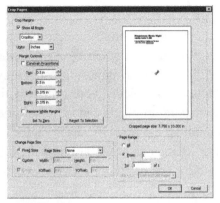

Fix Hairlines

Hairlines in PDF documents can be a little difficult to control and manipulate because they are so thin. When you preview your document with decreased magnification level, it can be easy to miss hairlines. You can use the Fix Hairlines tool to replace hairlines with thicker lines.

Figure 11-21

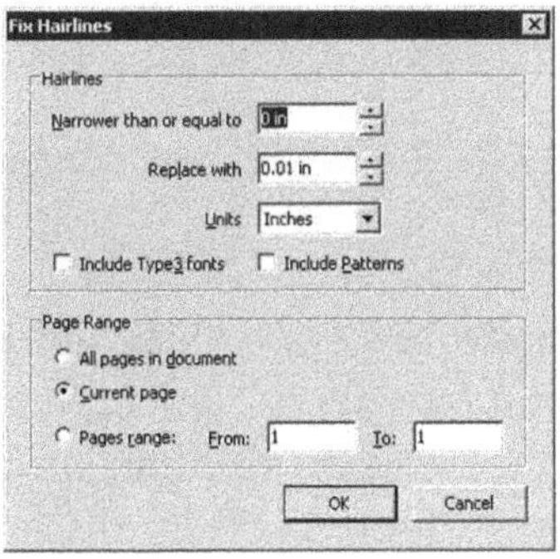

Transparency Flattening

When your document contains transparent objects, you usually need to flatten them before you submit your document to print press because not all programs support transparency. Without flattening your transparent objects, your output will be hard to predict—the transparent objects can be misaligned, for example. You can adjust the level of raster/vector balance and other transparency settings and then preview the effects of these changes by using the Flattener Preview window.

Figure 11-22

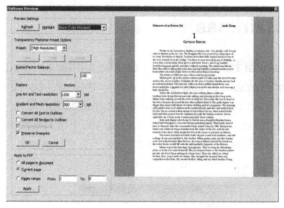

PDF Optimizer

The PDF Optimizer window gives you numerous options to analyze, modify, and optimize your document for smaller file size and better performance. It is divided into six categories: images, fonts, transparency, discard objects, discard user data, and clean up. Each category give you a number of options to optimize your PDF document.

Figure 11-23

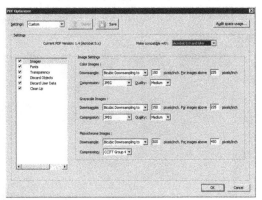

JDF Job Definitions

JDF file is being used for information exchange among different applications and systems for designer, prepress, and production in the graphic, art, print, and design areas. JDF is based on XML. Inside JDF, you can specify your print job definitions and production workflow. In addition, you can include PDF conversion and preflight properties for production process into JDF file. You can also save a set of JDF files as templates. Creating templates can save you time if you print similar materials over and over again.

Figure 11-24

You can click on the **Edit** button to make changes to your JDF file including general information and customer information.

Figure 11-25

Summary

In this chapter, we introduced the final stage of your PDF document—print and production. At the beginning of the chapter, we discussed how to print your document inside Adobe Acrobat. In addition, we covered Print Preset, how to print a selected area inside your document, and how to print bookmarks.

Later, we introduced eleven types of print production tools: Trap Presets, Output Preview, Preflight, Convert Colors, Ink Manager, Add Printer Marks, Crop Pages, Fix Hairlines, Flattener Preview, PDF Optimizer, and JDF Job Definitions. You can use these tools to manage ink and colors in your document, add printer marks such as trim, flatten transparent objects or artworks, trap presets, preview your document, examine preflight properties, optimize your document, and much more. These options are very powerful and they are also very helpful for your print production needs.

Appendix I

Install Adobe Acrobat 8 Professional

Installing Adobe Acrobat 8 Professional is an easy process. In this appendix, we will cover the typical installation process. You can install Adobe Acrobat 8 Professional from either CD or download it from the Adobe web site. Please note that to activate your production, you will need either a phone service or an Internet access.

 The only issue I have encountered during Adobe Acrobat installation was related Adobe Photoshop 7. If you have Adobe Photoshop 7 installed, installing Adobe Acrobat 8 Professional can disable Adobe Photoshop 7. Even after reinstall PhotoShop 7 on the same computer, the application still experiencing issues. If you install Adobe Acrobat 8 Professional on a machine has no Adobe Photoshop 7 installed, you can install Photoshop 7 after you have installed Adobe Acrobat 8 Professional, and the application should work as desired. The rule of thumb is, install Adobe Acrobat 8 Professional first, and then install Photoshop 7. If you have Photoshop 7 installed currently, you should uninstall it before installing Adobe Acrobat 8 Professional. There is no known issue with Photoshop CS3, however, so you should be able to install either application in any sequence.

System Requirements

Windows

Intel Pentium III processor or equivalent
Microsoft Windows 2000 with Service Pack 4; Windows
Server 2003 (32-bit or 64-bit editions) with Service Pack 1;
Windows XP Professional, Home, Tablet PC, or 64-bit Editions
with Service Pack 2; or Windows Vista Home Basic, Home
Premium, Ultimate, Business, or Enterprise (32-bit or 64-bit
editions)
Microsoft Internet Explorer 6 or 7
512MB of RAM or higher
1,360MB of available hard-disk space
1,024x768 screen resolution

Macintosh

PowerPC G3, G4, G5, or Intel processors
Mac OS X v.10.4.3
512MB of RAM or higher
1,060MB of available hard-disk space
1,024x768 screen resolution
DVD-ROM drive

Installation Process

You can start your installation process either from the product
CD or software download.

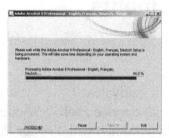

Once your installation process starts, you can choose your application language.

Enter user information and serial number (or using trial account).

Choose **Next** to continue.

You should see a list applications supported by Adobe Acrobat 8 Professional.

Select setup type: typical, complete, or custom.

Designate destination folder for your installation, by default it is:
C:\Program Files\Adobe\Acrobat 8\

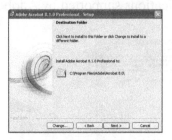

Once you click on **Next**, you should see ready to install screen.

Once you click **Install** button, your installation process starts. You should be able to see your installation progress from the status bar and the estimated remaining time.

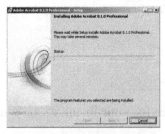

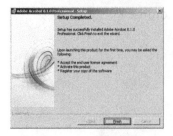

The first time when you log into Adobe Acrobat 8 Professional, you should see a user-friendly flash screen with most popular features.

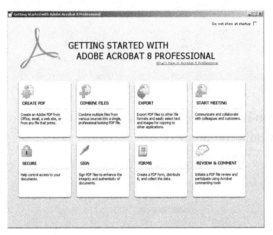

Installing SDK

Please note that you should download and install latest Adobe Acrobat SDK. Currently, the download web site address for SDK documentation is:

http://www.adobe.com/devnet/acrobat/

The download address for SDK executable program is:

http://www.adobe.com/support/downloads/thankyou.jsp?ftpID =3796&fileID=3537

Once you have successfully downloaded SDK, you can start your installation process.

When your installation process is completed, you should see the confirmation screen.

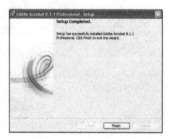

The Pocket Book of Adobe Acrobat 8 Professional

Index

T

vector, 79-80, 196
verify, 87, 137, 154
video, 163-169
visibility, 67
Visio, 42, 53

watermark, 56, 66-69
web, 73-80, 86, 156, 169
window, 17-21, 24, 26, 30-34, 49-51, 60-62, 88, 90-91, 102, 109, 113,
        122-125, 128, 130-131, 136, 138-139, 143, 146-148, 153, 155,
        158, 163-169, 171-173, 178-180, 184-186, 194, 201
wizard, 56
worksheet, 39-40, 59
workspace, 15-16, 33, 49-51, 86, 130
World Wide Web Consortium (W3C), 74

XML, 27-28, 71-75, 80, 110, 126-128, 197